LONGING FOR TENDERNESS
Responsible Love before Marriage

Gerhard Hauer

Foreword by
Ingrid Trobisch

Translated by Steven R. Palmer

InterVarsity Press
Downers Grove
Illinois 60515

Originally published as Sehnsucht nach Zärtlichkeit, © *1981 by Editions Trobisch, 7640 Kehl/Rhein, West Germany. All rights, including duplication and translation, reserved.*

English translation © *1983 by Gerhard Hauer, published in America by InterVarsity Press, Downers Grove, Illinois.*

All rights reserved. No part of this book may be reproduced in any form without written permission from InterVarsity Press, Downers Grove, Illinois.

InterVarsity Press is the book-publishing division of Inter-Varsity Christian Fellowship, a student movement active on campus at hundreds of universities, colleges and schools of nursing. For information about local and regional activities, write IVCF, 233 Langdon St., Madison, WI 53703.

Distributed in Canada through InterVarsity Press, 860 Denison St., Unit 3, Markham, Ontario L3R 4H1, Canada.

All biblical quotations are from the Revised Standard Version of the Bible, copyrighted 1946, 1952, © *1971, 1973.*

ISBN 0-87784-835-1

Printed in the United States of America

Library of Congress Cataloging in Publication Data

Hauer, Gerhard, 1943-
   Longing for tenderness.

   Translation of: Sehnsucht nach Zärtlichkeit.
   1. Love.   2. Tenderness (Psychology).   3. Sex.
I. Title
HQ801.H3613   1983   306.7'35   83-4304
ISBN 0-87784-835-1

16	15	14	13	12	11	10	9	8	7	6	5	4	3	2
95	94	93	92	91	90	89	88	87	86	85	84	83		

To everyone who longs for love

*In thankful remembrance of Walter Trobisch
and his tireless work to promote tender
and responsible love in friendship,
marriage and family.*

1.	A Universal Longing *11*
2.	Looking for Love *15*
3.	The Sexual Revolution and Tenderness *21*
4.	Sex before Marriage: Evaluating the Arguments *33*
5.	Warning—Danger Ahead *47*
6.	Choosing to Wait *67*
7.	Taking Stock *79*
8.	The Rewards of Tenderness *87*
9.	Hope for the Future *107*
10.	Christians, Tenderness and Sexuality *111*

Foreword

It is a pleasure for me to introduce this book to American readers. I have known Gerhard and Brigitte Hauer for several years and have worked with them in Family Life Seminars in Germany. Gerhard is a successful family counselor who knows what he is writing about.

Before my husband's sudden death in 1979, he had an opportunity to read this book while it was still in manuscript form. At that time, Walter urged publication, feeling that it would be a companion volume to his book *Living with Unfulfilled Desires*. Walter wrote to Gerhard: "I know how much deep thinking and intensive work you have put into this magnificent manuscript. You have succeeded in expressing yourself with clarity and simplicity. I can only congratulate you on the beauty of your language. I know how hard you have worked on it, for it is easy to read. Above all, you were wise to speak as a psychologist and psychotherapist and only in the last chapter to state your position as a Christian."

As a woman, I feel that often the longing for fulfillment can be more beautiful than the fulfillment itself. It is good to be thirsty, to look for tenderness. This is the deep longing, not only of youth, but of loving people of all ages. Gerhard writes: "Tenderness has an element of magic and mystery. As a blossom in a bud, it remains hidden from those who are impatient or possessive. But it reveals itself when it is honestly sought. . . . Tenderness can very quickly be overwhelmed by stormy sexuality. . . . Many who end up having sex were originally searching for tenderness. This book is a love letter: an invitation to experience tenderness."

Ingrid Trobisch

A Universal Longing
1

I am a sexual being and want to experience this sexuality fully." A fourteen-year-old boy hurled this sentence at the West German president and other dignitaries assembled in Bonn to open the International Year of the Child.

The boy continued, "I want to experience this sexuality with adults, with fourteen-year-olds, with sixteen-year-olds, with eighteen-year-olds, with boys and with girls, with men and with women. Sex and age do not matter. I need love more than anything else. And love is just what I don't get because other things are supposedly more important, other things like high school, college, studying and making money. Why can't I live what I feel?"

Much as we are taken aback by such a radical battle cry, we can still read in it the search for love. The boy says, "I need love more than anything else." He longs for tenderness but does not recognize the difference between a giving love and a love that demands its own way. He confuses his genuine need for affection and love with his supposed right to sexual satisfaction.

We all have a longing for tenderness, and we all have sexual needs. Erotic love is stronger and more demanding than tender, giving love: tenderness can very quickly be overwhelmed by stormy sexuality. Not surprisingly, young people have trouble controlling their desire for affection. Many who end up having sex were originally searching for tenderness.

In my practice as counselor and psychotherapist, I am confronted time and again with problems concerning love, tenderness and sexuality. I frequently see uncertainty and helplessness. For you who are questioning and searching, I would like to examine different views of sex outside marriage. In this way you can recognize in your own situation opportunities to make loving yet responsible decisions—both for yourself and for your partner. This book is directed toward young people and single, divorced or widowed adults; but parents, educators and counselors will also find suggestions for dealing with these difficult questions.

Love, tenderness and sexuality must be considered on their own terms, independently of what everyone's doing and what happens to be in. The Pill, petting and living together are all popular. All three ring with the promise of sexual freedom. But in more and more cases this offer of sexual liberation has led to enslavement and dependence.

This book says no to irresponsible sexuality as well as to inhibition, prudery and false guilt feelings. It says no both to the easy answers of petting and living together, and to empty moralizing. Its message is a definite yes to sexuality: an expectant yes to a tender and responsible use of this natural and exciting life force. It is my goal to encourage you to find your own path. This book is a love letter: an invitation to experience tenderness.

I am a psychologist and psychotherapist. I have been married since 1969 and have two children. We live consciously as a Christian family, and we want to make our experiences available to others.

I am intentionally forgoing the security of a long bibliography. This book is based on many personal conversations and experiences, from either my profession or my personal life, and does not rely on opinion polls or experimental results for support. In my opinion, the topics of tenderness and sexuality are much too intimate to be captured in the statistical analysis of a systematic opinion poll. Reports of that type are always available in bookstores. Personal opinions and experiences are more in demand today.

I encourage you to prepare to analyze your thoughts honestly, because that is the only way to discover the longing for tenderness.

Looking for Love
2

Ron and Jacqueline saw each other for the first time on their way to school. He was electrified as his glance happened to meet her dark eyes. She was standing at the bus stop in front of City Hall, passing time by watching the crowds. She hesitated as their eyes met. "Nice looking," she thought. "Too bad he was looking at the same time! Now he probably thinks I like him." If Jacqueline had paid better attention to her feelings, she would have noticed that this chance meeting had left her surprisingly excited.

Indeed there were a number of feelings at work in her. She felt as if she had been caught watching him and was ashamed of her curiosity. At the same time she was annoyed at the unabashed way a strange guy had taken such a long look at her. It was a good thing she had looked away quickly, or he might have thought she was flirting with him. She could be glad that he hadn't come over to talk to her. But was that really good luck? He looked rather nice, and he didn't look pushy at all. What can a girl do? If you're too careful you look proud or shy, and then no one comes near you. But as soon as you respond a little, a lot of guys think they can get away with almost anything and even start to dream of going to bed.

Ron was thinking similar thoughts as he went on his way. It was probably because of his uncertainty that he didn't turn around a single time. "Whether you're forward or reserved," he thought, "you are going to be misunderstood."

Neither of them could forget this chance meeting of the eyes. Jacqueline remembered Ron's face in all kinds of different situations. During class Ron daydreamed of Jacqueline's enchanting dark eyes. A short time later Ron sauntered past the City Hall bus stop. The place where she had stood, he noticed, was empty. Just as he was about to walk by, he caught a glimpse of her through the window of a stopped bus. He was petrified. With pounding heart he stepped forward. Her right hand was pressed against the glass as she leaned on the window. Ron could see the creases in her palm. She still hadn't noticed him. He felt a rush of happiness that her hand was so near. Spontaneously he pressed his hand on the same space on the outside of the glass. She jumped and pulled her hand away as if she had actually been touched.

Frightened, they looked into each other's eyes. Was this touch through the window glass too daring? With the exchanged glance, each gently tested the genuineness and trustworthiness of the other. And then suddenly, like the sun breaking through the clouds, something tender flashed through their suspicion. They smiled at each other affectionately. Before long Ron and Jacqueline were dating steadily.

One day they went to a swimming pool near the woods. Since there were long lines waiting for the changing booths and they were in a hurry, Jacqueline decided to change her clothes in the bushes. She asked Ron to hold up a blanket to give her some privacy. It would have been easy for him to sneak a look as she changed her clothes. The very thought excited him. But then he thought of the natural and unembarrassed way that Jacqueline had asked him for his help. Suddenly he realized that his sexual curiosity had almost caused him to commit a serious breach of trust. On the way home the two talked about their shared experience. They found that Ron's self-control had increased their trust for one another.

Ron and Jacqueline's friendship was soon taken for granted by the people around them. Their parents and friends were happy with their stable, trusting relationship. Everyone assumed that they would take a vacation trip together the summer after they met. Among their friends, many couples went camping together and slept together alone in a tent. Should they do the same? Ron and Jacqueline talked about their fears and expectations. Certainly by now it would be okay. They both knew exactly what they wanted from their relationship. And everyone could see at a glance that they weren't just after sex but that they were loving and responsible.

But Ron and Jacqueline began to have second thoughts. They saw how tempting it would be to sleep so close to one another in the shelter of the tent. Even though they had agreed before the vacation not to have intimate relations, each would feel the warm closeness of the other. Each of them had often secretly wished to yield completely to the other and had intuitively sensed that the other felt the same way. They sensed that it would be too much of a strain to lie next to each other night after night, longing for tenderness and intimacy while practicing strict self-control. They knew that in a loving relationship it makes no sense to torment each other with closeness just to prove they can get through without yielding to temptation. Their solution was to find another couple with the same vacation plans and double up, girls in one tent, boys in the other.

Ron and Jacqueline, though engaged after high school, did not have intimate relations until they were married three years later. By the time they married, they had built up a great reserve of shared experience in loving and considerate treatment of one another. With this background they could master the conflicts and crises that they encountered in marriage, and they could pass on to the next generation a legacy of tenderness. Their children often observe their parents flirting with each other. As a result of the tender and responsible way the parents treat one another, the children also look forward to one day meeting a partner and marrying.

Responsible tenderness is infrequent nowadays, and to some this love story may seem to be just a fantasy. Others may object that it sounds too idealistic and utopian. Who in today's society could live up to such an ideal? Yet Ron and Jacqueline, though their names have been changed, are real people, and a tender and responsible love relationship is a real possibility even today. But there are two prerequisites: age and maturity.

The first prerequisite is physical: age! When Ron and Jacqueline met they were eighteen and sixteen. Ron was four years older than the fourteen-year-old boy whose speech so bluntly favored sexual freedom. And although Ron and Jacqueline were not children when they met, they waited four more years—until they had reached full adulthood—before marrying and enjoying intimate relations.

But even more important than age is maturity, the maturity which sees the need for responsibility in tenderness. (Of course maturity is related to age.) Let's fade back to the romance of Ron and Jacqueline. Although they did not engage in sexual intercourse, they obviously experienced sexual needs. It is also obvious that they did not stand passively by and let the events carry them along. On the contrary, they both invested a great deal of energy and patience in building their relationship. If Ron had been content with his daydreams and if Jacqueline had only admired Ron from a distance, then they would have built nothing but individual dream worlds. They would not have taken advantage of their opportunity to get to know each other and to use their sexuality with tenderness and responsibility.

In spite of the strong sex drive, almost everyone longs first for tenderness and love. Many young people, like the fourteen-year-old boy at the beginning of the chapter, are actually searching for love and not primarily for sex. They are looking for trust and human closeness. Probably everyone hopes for a relationship full of love and tenderness, a relationship to which both partners contribute openness, trust, fairness, tact and loyalty.

But between a person's wish for tenderness and his or her actual behavior lies a world of difference. Everyone longs for tenderness, but only a few are prepared to meet the prerequisites.

It makes me very sad when I see children, young people and even adults knowingly walking into unhappiness because they apply the examples set for them in film, television and the press too early or one-sidedly. They learn about sex appeal but not about tender and responsible sexuality. It hurts to see young people with hard and cynical eyes—already exploited and used up by the age of eighteen. They have lost their youthful beauty before they ever had a chance to mature.

A great share of the guilt for this tragic development is borne by the so-called sexual revolution.

The Sexual Revolution and Tenderness
3

Tenderness is threatened by the sexual revolution. For many readers this idea will be disturbing. It sounds like a contradiction. How can I speak disparagingly of the sexual revolution when love is what it's all about? Isn't it cruel to deny physical intimacy to people who are in love? It is common knowledge that a great percentage of young people have had intimate sexual experiences. Many are sleeping together and most are familiar with petting. We are living in a time when open and honest discussion of sexuality is leading to emancipation. Thanks to the sexual enlightenment, today's young people masturbate without guilt feelings. Plenty of options are available for satisfying sexual needs with or without a partner. Many explicit books on sex techniques and many aids for all kinds of sexual problems are available.

Many psychologists emphasize how important it is to recognize needs and to satisfy them. If I don't agree with such thinking, am I perhaps sexually inhibited? Or am I trying to impose my morals on others, afraid of the power and depth of sexuality? Or am I just envious of those who are enjoying life?

These are common arguments. For several years in newspapers, books, films and discussions we have seen an upsurge of sexual liberation. One fortunate result is that now sex can be discussed as openly and honestly as any other matter. Prudery and sexual taboos have lost a lot of ground. We have replaced untruthfulness and inhibition with openness and spontaneity. In many cases this has improved marital relationships and helped promote honest discussions with children and young people.

The negative side effects of this freedom and liberalization, however, are numerous, and they are at least as harmful as the dishonest prudery of earlier times. Billboard pictures and captions aim to awaken sexual needs without any reference to tenderness and love. Pornographic films openly propagate perversion and brutality. Advertisements in newspapers and magazines are no longer merely suggestive: the overwhelming majority emphasize the interest in purely sensual pleasure.

The opportunities for sexual contact are abundant, whether through "massage parlors" or mate-swapping or gay bars. Sex shops offer a wide selection: Besides the usual pornography in picture, film and literature, there is an electric dildo that represents an unequivocal invitation to masturbation for lonely or neglected women. For men there is even an inflatable playmate, "life-like, life-size, flexible. . . . Blow her up and you have a beautiful playmate with ideal measurements, warm, soft, made of flesh-colored vinyl, a thousand and one possibilities. You pay only $25.00."

The fact that this advertisement did not appear in a pornographic magazine, but in a widely read periodical, indicates the general acceptance of the sexual revolution. Such manifestations of the sexual revolution arouse curiosity about atypical and abnormal behavior in love and sexual relationships. Our society is being programmed with nothing less than a subliminal seduction to perversion. Those who play down such aberrations deceive themselves when they believe that the only people affected are old bachelors and lonely eccentrics. No one who goes through life with open eyes and ears can escape the influence of the sexual revolution. Unfortunately, the value of the sexual revolution—greater openness and less inhibition—is relatively small. The harm, however, is great. Today's expectations of sexual fulfillment grow boundlessly and overwhelm feelings of tenderness before they can grow and develop. The violent sexual revolution destroys budding trust, security, responsibility and love.

The sexual revolution has several characteristics: overemphasized needs, a consumer mentality, one-sided sex education and blind faith in statistics. Let's examine each one more closely.

The Tyranny of Needs

Needs are certainly normal and important. Our needs to eat, drink and sleep keep us alive. Furthermore, needs are the engine that drive our entire behavior. They make our lives interesting and give them warmth. They are important even to people who have not learned to take them seriously. Inhibited people who suppress their own opinions and do not stand up for their own rights must learn to perceive and express their needs. People with sexual inhibitions must learn to recognize their sexual needs as normal and valuable, though manageable.

Satisfying legitimate needs must be distinguished from pursuing satisfaction at any cost, that is, making the need an absolute and denying all boundaries. To live for one's needs without consideration for others or for one's own responsibility must necessarily lead to spiritual neglect and to chaos in society. When needs are overemphasized, values are endangered.

One such endangered value is modesty, important because it protects our privacy. Under the tyranny of sexual needs, healthy feelings of modesty are devalued and cast aside as inhibitions. A twenty-year-old woman told me that after a party she decided to spend the night in the same living room with three young men. The three men undressed in her presence without hesitation, but she waited until she could turn out the light. She later related this experience to a friend, who was surprised to hear how inhibited she had been. The woman was shocked by her friend's response. She thought that by spending the night in the same room with three men she had proved that she was not burdened by inhibitions.

Once modesty, shyness and reservation are branded as inhibitions, they are effectively dismissed. Who wants to be inhibited or old-fashioned? Sexual needs can be fully expressed in our present society with small risk of rebuff or reprimand. Against the background of a sexually permissive society, peer pressure can become so strong that the only escape is to go forward under the mottos "Keep up with the times!" and "No inhibitions!" Life can be difficult for teen-agers who refuse to participate in sex games at parties or adults who balk at "group therapy" or "sensitivity training" sessions which use specifically sexual "nonverbal exercises." Great inner conflicts develop when the boundary between abnormal inhibitions and healthy modesty is erased. The push for sexual freedom can destroy healthy and valuable feelings of modesty.

Those who act only in response to their immediate needs neglect their responsibility for solving problems and end up making hasty decisions. The slogan "A woman should have control of her own body" is often cited as sufficient justification for an abortion. An individual's right to develop his own personality is exaggerated and possibly used to justify a divorce. These are abuses of needs. Values such as modesty or fidelity or the sanctity of human life are destroyed when needs become the basis for decision making. When sexual needs are overemphasized, the ability to experience tenderness and love is lost.

Sex in a Consumer Society

Today's consumer mentality is closely related to the overemphasis on needs. Advertisers work hard to stimulate and strengthen feelings of need. Even luxury items are presented as being vitally important. We often recognize this extensive manipulation of our needs and tastes, but we nevertheless end up adopting the fashion we once found ridiculous. This vicious circle of consumerism involves several factors: abundance, immoderation, superficiality and the disruption of natural rhythms.

We live amid an *abundance* of consumer goods. Any people in the Western world can afford almost anything they want, whether a luxurious car, a fantastic vacation trip or an expensive hobby. Stores are brimming with products. Sales seduce us to come and buy. This oversupply also holds true for sexual consumerism. Tenderness is pushed aside more and more while sex, purely physical satisfaction, is promoted ever more openly and shamelessly.

We respond to the abundance of consumer goods with *immoderation*. We want to have more and more from life. We continue to chase after consumer goods even when we already feel that they do not make us happy. We have no more time for the pleasure of anticipation, especially in the case of holidays such as birthdays, Easter and particularly Christmas. Instead of the joy of the occasion, we experience only greater stress. We also have no more time to savor the happy memories of what we have experienced. The next deadline or yet another diversion demands our attention, but again only for a short time. Immoderation also exists for sexuality. Consumption without leisure destroys what is exciting and beautiful. A vicious circle? It would sometimes seem to be a prison from which there is no escape.

All this results in *superficiality*. There is never time to deepen anything: professions, interpersonal relationships or even hobbies. With so many ways to spend free time, people often have several hobbies without having enough time for any of them. Superficiality automatically results. Sexual activity outside a responsible, tender relationship is also superficial. The appetite for excitement grows and grows until it reaches perversion. Love and tenderness hardly stand a chance.

The final component of the vicious circle is *the disruption of natural rhythms*. Nature is outwitted so that people might have anything at any time. People can turn summer into winter by traveling to high-elevation ski resorts, and they can leave the cold of winter to bask in the Caribbean. Thanks to the freezer, fresh strawberries can appear on the table at any time. The excitement that comes from the anticipation of unfulfilled wishes is lost. Consumerism guarantees that almost everything is available and that hardly anyone needs to wait for anything.

Fashion has also leveled the differences between the sexes. Women wear slacks, vests and man-tailored shirts. When a woman dressed this way walks ahead of you beside a long-haired man, it is hardly possible to distinguish the sexes at a distance. Fortunately many natural rhythms such as day and night and rain and drought are beyond our control. The more we level, the more we equalize differences, the more boring our lives become. This is also true of sexuality. The simulated pregnancy created by the Pill interrupts the natural alternation of fertile and infertile days. Some men brutally conclude that women are always available. Is this progress for tenderness and love, or even for eroticism and sexuality?

In spite of all our insight we find it difficult to escape the attitude of consumerism. Sex, even the pursuit of sexual satisfaction as a consumer article, can always be hidden behind the word *love*. Furthermore, sexual consumerism is not limited to sex-film afficionados and sex-shop customers; rather it is promoted by the omnipresent communications media. We need only think of magazine covers, suggestive advertisements or screaming newspaper headlines. Many readers' interest is aroused especially quickly and thoroughly by reports of criminal sexual offenses. A detailed description of a rape gives these readers exactly what they want.

In spite of its pervasiveness, our throw-away consumer society does not make people happy. Sex as a consumer article does not satisfy. We all know, or at least somehow feel, that immoderation poisons the joy of life. When someone wants only to possess, the ability to experience tenderness is lost—and the loss is immeasurable. A yes to pleasure coupled with a no to responsibility spells the end not only for tenderness but for humanity itself.

One-sided Sex Education

I am fully in favor of sex education when it means the open discussion of sexual questions in the family or in school in a way that is appropriate to the age group. A proven guideline is to answer all the child's questions—no less but no more. In this way children can set the pace for their own education. It is a tragedy when children must secretly learn what they can about the body and sexuality from an encyclopedia or on the street.

It is becoming increasingly hard to inform children about sex at the right time, however, because puberty is starting at an ever earlier age in both boys and girls. Many a nine- or ten-year-old girl is already so well developed that she looks like a woman and is attractive to boys and even men. I know a young woman who first had sexual intercourse at the age of twelve and who by the age of fourteen was expecting her first child. Her case is especially disturbing because from the very beginning she could not meet the demands placed on her. Even today because of her young age she has great difficulty in fulfilling her roles as wife, homemaker and mother. As a result both of her children have spent time in a foster home. A timely explanation of sexual matters might have averted this tragedy. Yet when sex education is given without consideration of values and morals, it can lead to sad results.

Rarely do today's efforts in sex education have loving relationships or responsible tenderness as their goal. For example, a widely distributed manual with very erotic pictures covering the topic of premarital pregnancy does not worry about how such situations come to be; rather sexual relationships between young people are taken for granted. This document limits its discussion to an exhaustive description of all available contraceptives, reducing the question of responsibility to one of being ready to prevent the conception of a child.

Statistics and Peer Pressure

A fourth characteristic of the sexual revolution is its blind faith in statistics. Numbers by their nature appear scientifically objective, valid and reliable, and scientific inquiries and opinion-poll results are especially convincing when they are presented in the form of statistics. Statistical results represent norms to which people, at least in cases of doubt, can conform. The norm shows what people usually do—in other words, what is normal. The implied slogan behind the use of many statistics is, "If everyone is doing it, it can't be wrong."

Who can escape the impression left by the statistics published by sex researchers? The majority of unmarried persons have sexual experience. The majority of married persons have not always been faithful to their spouses. Such high percentages are not a phenomenon of the last few years alone, so why all the fuss today if people have thought this way about sexual relationships for many years?

In earlier years when a couple had premarital relations it was with the understanding that they were acting contrary to the norm.

The term *premarital sex* emphasizes this: sexual union, though it can be experienced before marriage, is normally identified with the marital relationship.

But the publication of statistics on sexual behavior seemed to shift the norms toward increasing sexual liberation. Now everyone could read how everyone else, according to opinion polls, was behaving sexually. This basically neutral information lost its neutrality by being published. It is only a small step from knowing what "everyone" is thinking or doing to turning this information into a compulsory standard, a "new morality." Here are some relevant examples from my counseling practice:

A well-developed thirteen-year-old girl told me matter-of-factly that by the age of eleven she was already being pursued by young men. "Of course," she said, she had "slept" with some of them. She reported this so openly that it was obvious that she found it completely normal.

A similar attitude surfaced in a dialog with fourteen- to eighteen-year-old young people. At the beginning of the evening each was allowed to write down any question on the topic "Sexuality and Love" and to turn it in unsigned. It was my job to answer the questions. Many wanted to know when it is okay to have sexual intercourse with a boyfriend or girlfriend and which contraceptive is best. A great share of the young people present took it for granted that "everyone" was sleeping together and that "everyone" was of course also using the Pill or some other contraceptive. They were shocked when I told them that my answers to these questions would be short, because I believe physical union belongs in marriage.

A teen-age girl came to a counseling appointment wearing a thin silk halter top. I remarked that her skimpy attire must certainly attract a lot of attention from the boys. She answered promptly that she had already slept with several boys. For her the usual way to get a boyfriend was to let him run his hand up her sweater or down her blouse.

A girl of almost thirteen with thoughts of suicide was brought to the school counseling service by her mother. The girl mentioned that she had to have sexual intercourse before her thirteenth birthday. Her girlfriend, who was one year older and had already slept with several partners, had impressed upon her that without sexual experience by thirteen she would be a failure. The girl was so convinced of this "norm" that she was ready to take any man as a partner.

The sexual revolution has also changed mothers' attitudes. That is the only way I can explain the fact that the mother of a pregnant fifteen-year-old told all her friends of her daughter's condition and happily explained that there were eleven men who were possible fathers. She was quite proud that her daughter "got around so much."

Many parents who would be appalled at that mother's attitude nevertheless have no objections when their teen-agers want to go camping with other young people—even though they are planning to have boys and girls sleep together in the same tent. Yet just such an intimate camping trip can begin an approach to sex that is fearfully deficient in both tenderness and responsibility.

In many cases the term *peer pressure* applies. This mysterious and brutal norm forces many to do what "everyone else is doing" even if it contradicts their own feelings and beliefs. In a survey of twenty-five prospective kindergarten teachers, fifteen had decided upon graduation from college to move in with their boyfriends, and five feared, some of them greatly, that they were abnormal because they didn't have boyfriends (the remaining five were already married). Peer pressure can pervert the joy of sexuality and make it into a performance test of sexual skill. Once again tenderness—a factor that cannot appear in statistics —loses out.

This blind trust in statistics betrays a great uncertainty about what sexual behavior is normal and what is abnormal. This uncertainty touches many people, even those who previously had a firm opinion. It took me two years to find my position. For a long time I was torn: I appreciated the sexual revolution's attention to human needs, but I observed many bitter experiences of young people and unmarried adults for whom sexual freedom had brought great emotional problems that would affect them the rest of their lives. On the one hand, the demand for more openness and education in sexual matters is certainly justified, and the sex drive is natural and completely normal. Yet on the other hand, gratification of the sex drive may make it particularly difficult to fulfill the longing for tenderness—another natural human need. It is certainly not surprising that people wonder where affection and sexuality mingle and why a distinction between them is necessary.

If we look closely at the characteristics of the sexual revolution, we may find, perhaps to our amazement, a side of ourselves! It is the part of us that seeks immediate satisfaction of our needs and that risks exaggerating them, that has succumbed to the consumer mentality, and that always wants to be up to date, doing what everyone else is doing.

Fortunately there is another side of us as well: that part of us that is willing and able to perceive ourselves as we are and to criticize ourselves honestly. Such honest self-analysis helps us in our struggle with those influences of the sexual revolution that would control us. It enables us to realistically assess our fears and desires in the area of sexuality.

Sex before Marriage: Evaluating the Arguments
4

A great percentage of young people and unmarried adults have experience in petting and sleeping together. Although this is widely accepted, rarely does anyone discuss the reasons motivating young people and adults to enter an intimate sexual relationship outside marriage. Instead of building a case for premarital sexual involvement, proponents are as likely to disparage that "superfluous legal document," the marriage license.

Let us recover lost ground and carefully examine the reasons for intimacy among young and unmarried people.

Doing What Comes Naturally

"The sex drive is a basic, natural need that demands satisfaction. This need is a given and is unaffected by age, by sex or by law, custom and morality." Somehow this statement sounds convincing, just like its logical conclusion, "So it is unnatural and inhuman to block the sex drive. If there is an opportunity to satisfy sexual need, use it!"

But the love act is neither a consumer article nor a sport. Anyone who oversimplifies sex as a typically human and irresistible phenomenon of nature will soon fit Eugen Roth's brilliant description in his poem "The Waster" (from *Mensch zu Mensch,* Büchergilde Gutenberg, Frankfurt):

His love affairs they came and went
He never knew quite what they meant
The love came unexpectedly
That is what love is meant to be.
The man searched deep within his soul
Where love had been he found a hole.

Tragically, such a "waster" can fool everyone and even himself or herself by disguising selfishness as love.

Some see sexual experience as a means of physical self-confirmation. Puberty occurs as early as age nine or ten with many girls and as early as twelve with boys, a full ten years before marriage is appropriate. Many young people want to get acquainted with these new possibilities and try them out early. Only those who have experienced a physical confirmation of their masculinity or femininity can develop a normal self-concept, some believe. Twelve-year-old Sylvia was undoubtedly curious and probably wanted to confirm her own sexuality as well. She thought it would be fun to break up her girlfriend's relationship with a fifteen-year-old boy by sleeping with him, something her girlfriend was not ready to do.

Others argue that early intimate contacts can be a defense

against the egocentric habit of masturbation, which can inhibit the development of a healthy self-concept as well as natural contact with members of the opposite sex. Such contacts also help to break home ties and thus offer opportunities to develop self-sufficiency, self-confidence and responsibility.

At first glance these arguments look sound. But early satisfaction of sexual needs gives only the initial appearance of success. The small advantage of having had a little more sexual experience is overshadowed by great disadvantages. Once the irreplaceable time of waiting and courting is lost, tenderness and sexuality have no opportunity to develop, and the need for consideration, caring and responsibility is greatly diminished. The "relationship" can be the cover for a monstrous selfishness: the desire to satisfy one's own sexual needs without waiting. This selfish attitude is obvious whether couples pet to climax or engage in sexual intercourse.

Some young people use sexual experience as a means to freedom. Some have even tried to get away from home by having a baby. As understandable as this desire for freedom is, it is a bad reason for having sex or getting married. Through my work as a counselor, I know several young families for which this great responsibility came too soon. Early marriages made only for the sake of the expected child often end in divorce a few years later.

An Educational Experience
The desire for practical experience sounds reasonable and even responsible. Isn't it clear that premarital experience could be useful in a later marriage? Couldn't it make the difference between confidence and clumsiness in intimate moments? Besides, someone who has already "sowed his wild oats" and satisfied his curiosity would more likely have the maturity necessary to choose a marriage partner. Early sexual experience would give freedom from the influence of purely sexual attraction. Sexual needs would no longer blur one's vision to real values, such as personality.

In practice this plausible argumentation all too quickly becomes carte blanche. Proponents of "sex for experience" are silent about the following problems: experiences limited to sex only increase the appetite for new excitement. They make any one partner seem boring. Purely superficial sex soon becomes monotonous, and the only promise of change lies in a new relationship. There is the danger that superficiality will become a conditioned response in all male-female relationships. Any hope of depth is lost this way—as with "the waster" in Roth's poem.

But someone may object, "What you say is true for promiscuous sex, but not for engaged couples. Ideally the first sexual intimacy is experienced in a relationship that is already stable and responsible. This is certainly an entirely different matter, especially if the partners plan to marry later."

Real life experiences contradict this assertion. A marriage cannot be tried out, not even by living together. Attitudes and feelings are necessarily much different before marriage—the final, public commitment to one person—than afterward. Experience shows that a trial marriage does not make the final decision to marry any easier, but rather makes it more difficult.

Love: Finding and Keeping It

The desire for love is the main motivation for most relationships. This desire takes two directions. The first is the need for warmth, closeness, security and tenderness, and the second is the need for praise, recognition and esteem. Obviously many people hope to fulfill all these needs in a relationship with another person.

Since every physical contact is by nature personal, physical closeness is particularly satisfying. A positive physical experience can make a partner's entire personality seem pleasant. But often these "obvious" conclusions later reveal themselves as horrible disappointments, particularly since the transitions from tender touch to mechanical sex may be indistinct. It is a mistake to engage in sexual intercourse in the hope of finding love.

It is especially tragic when a person enters into a sexual relationship with the honest desire to help someone in need. Physical union, or at least petting, is supposed to prove that the offer to help is serious, to "seal" the relationship with a commitment to stick together through thick and thin. Perhaps this deeply shared sexual experience will also help the other to escape his or her problems.

This desire to help a partner out of his or her troubles can be the beginning of horrible tragedies. I think specifically of those young people who want to help an alcoholic or a drug addict escape dependency. The noble desire of one partner to help and the resulting pressure on the other to succeed set up the relationship for disappointment and heartbreak. In my opinion physical union plays a special role here. Disappointment is especially great after sexual submission because this proof of the helper's sincerity was expected to bring immediate and visible success.

The sexual union that was thought to insure success soon turns into a shackle from which there is no escape. Many helpers, plagued by guilt feelings, do not leave even when the sick partner clings self-pityingly and complainingly to his or her "victim" role and emotionally exhausts everyone. Instead of healing for the sick partner, the result is often an unhealthy mutual dependence. Sensitive people with strong social values are especially susceptible to such a tragic helper "career." It cannot be emphasized enough: Establishing a sexual relationship for the purpose of helping one's partner does not liberate him but rather leads him—and his helper—into a new dependence.

While some people enter into a sexual relationship to find love, others do so to keep the love they have found. Lovers obviously want to belong to one another totally and to share themselves with one another in every way, including physically. In petting and in physical union affection is experienced firsthand. This sharing is supposed to provide security and to prove how serious the friendship is. The lovers may hope that these intimate experiences will make the relationship even more stable and secure.

Many observations contradict this belief. Intimate contacts often make people less rather than more certain. Inexperience and clumsy behavior in the first sexual contact can cause tensions that are easier to deal with in the stable relationship of marriage. High expectations make disappointment inevitable. The man in particular is subject to a paradoxical change of moods. Even though he was the one who pushed so hard for sexual intimacy, once he has gotten what he wanted he is often disappointed over the woman's unexpectedly quick compliance. And the woman in turn is disappointed with herself for giving in too soon. Each may resent the other for assuming too little responsibility. In any case greater insecurity rather than increased stability is likely to result.

Love cannot be proved but can only be experienced. Love thrives on trust. Security can grow only if the partners trust each other. But especially in those relationships where petting and sleeping together is the norm, trust can be undermined at any time by the pointed question, "Is the real reason for our intimacy simply selfishness, the desire to possess?"

Fear

All the motives for sexual involvement we have looked at so far arise from needs, whether physical, intellectual, emotional or even spiritual. Many people, however, are sexually active not from need but from fear. Fear as a motivator can make a person dependent and mold his or her life. Many people, for example, will go further sexually than they really want to out of fear of losing a beloved partner.

Fear can be long-lived and difficult to get rid of. Learning theory has a good explanation of this. As a rule, fear causes pain which leads to an avoidance or flight reaction. Behavior that avoids pain will tend to become more frequent. Many people, fearful of loneliness or rejection, try to escape through premature intimate relations. Running from their fear, they become more and more sexually active—even though this behavior does not bring happiness but only delays pain. Fear is pushed into the background for a short time, but it will soon be back in full strength.

Many different fears urge people into premature sexual relationships: fear of physical deterioration and emotional abnormality, fear of loneliness, fear that time is running out, fear of coercion, fear of causing pain.

People with *fear of physical deterioration* are afraid that normal bodily functions may "get rusty" if they are not used. Men fear impotence and women fear frigidity. This fear is becoming more widespread as the time lengthens between puberty and the conclusion of education. Today's extended adolescence creates genuine problems for young people in dealing with their physical needs and tensions. Some decide that it is better to have sex than to get sick or masturbate. Yet no medical evidence indicates that sexual abstinence should cause concern for physical well-being. On the contrary, the man's nocturnal ejaculation regulates his system naturally and automatically. The fear of physical deterioration is thus an unrealistic nightmare, lacking any scientific basis.

Next to the fear of physical strain there is, particularly among well-educated and open-minded young people, the *fear of emotional abnormality*. These young people fear not only impotence and frigidity, but also sexual perversions if their sex drive is not satisfied and allowed to develop. At best the result would be regular masturbation that could finally become an addiction. They conclude, "It would be better to permit premarital relations and even to promote them!"

Sexual disturbances do not result from sexual inexperience, but from denying sexuality or even thinking it to be evil. Sexual abnormalities do not result from waiting voluntarily. Conscious relinquishment pending the final decision for a life partner does no harm. On the contrary, waiting brings advantages—and very great ones. The older a couple are, the more mature they are likely to be and the more genuine and certain their reasons for marrying.

Of course a running battle between sexual needs and self-control is no solution! Neither is consistently suppressing and denying sexual needs. There is only one way to deal with sexuality: for both partners to decide to put up with natural tensions while practicing tenderness and responsibility in their relationship.

This ability to put up with tensions is the mark of a mature person. Emotional and intellectual development is possible only when people learn to control the impulsive nature of their needs. Drives should not be the lord and master of the individual; the individual should be in control. Only those who have themselves in hand, who practice self-control and who can "do without" are able to learn values like care and responsibility and to change impulsive sexuality into tenderness and partnership.

The ability to love must be learned. It takes time. The person who allows himself or herself time to learn tenderness and the responsible management of sexuality has a greater chance of founding a happy marriage with a like-minded partner, because the person who has learned to love can, through love, change others.

We all know of someone who was changed through loving or being loved. This is true not only of lovers, but also of the depressed adult who is made to laugh by a happy child, of the unattractive person who blossoms in a love relationship, or of lifeless eyes that sparkle again. A love attack works like magic, changing both the lover and the beloved.

It is not necessary to make a checklist and search the world for the ideal life's partner. Instead, we can practice love and tenderness in any situation, in all interpersonal relationships and even in the treatment of animals. This force of love can and will change people, not through demands and reproofs but through an ever-widening wave of tenderness.

The *fear of loneliness* is also a frequent reason for entering into an intimate relationship. A young man is sexually excited and strongly desires physical contact with his new girlfriend. Out of fear of losing her boyfriend, the young woman gives in. Situations like this are especially likely if the young man expects or even demands sexual intimacy as an indication or proof of the young woman's love. In such cases the woman will often give in even if she has misgivings. Fear of losing their boyfriends motivates many young women to engage in petting or even intercourse.

This fear of loneliness is significant in other situations as well. For example, people who are "living together" often fear separation. Even if the relationship has already become boring or cool, the partners stay together out of fear of the loneliness that would follow separation. In the worst case one partner may even decide to hold onto the other by having a child.

I have observed that the fear of loneliness is especially prevalent among girls and women. As a rule, men are more active than women in their search for a partner. For this reason it is easier for a man to initiate an acquaintance without making a bad impression. On the other hand, a woman risks all kinds of misunderstandings if she takes the initiative. Since women and girls have a more difficult time finding a new partner after a separation, their greater fear of being alone is understandable. But those who give in to this fear of loneliness run the risk of becoming unhealthily dependent. They necessarily lose the opportunity for maturation that can be realized only in self-sufficiency and freedom.

Another motive for premarital sex is the *fear that time is running out.* Young people and single adults, constantly confronted with sex in word and picture, may begin to panic if they see no chance of finally having a sexual relationship. These fears are worsened by the sexual standards set by many magazines. Anyone who does not want to be branded a prude soon adopts the motto, "It's better to find anyone right away than no one at all!" Standards for picking a partner are lowered bit by bit until an acceptable partner comes along who is ready for petting and then for bed.

A young woman who had already been involved in many intimate relationships told me that around the age of thirteen or fourteen, as the result of reading a magazine for teen-agers, she began to feel abnormal: she had no boyfriend. At seventeen she finally had intercourse for the first time, but at the expense of a guilty conscience. She pushed these feelings aside, commenting that she was still annoyed at the prudish way her mother had raised her.

Those who respond to peer pressure and the fear that time is running out surrender control of a very personal area of their lives to outside forces. Whereas once many people were captive to a prudish attitude toward sexuality, today just as many are captive to the extreme opposite attitude, sexual license. Instead of finding liberation they hop out of the frying pan and into the fire, from an old prison into a new one.

Particularly horrible is the *fear of coercion*. This fear results from a relationship in which the man puts extreme pressure on the woman to give in to his need for sexual contact, even though she does not want it. The pressure may consist of threats of physical abuse or of circulating rumors that would destroy the woman's reputation. Coercion of this sort borders on blackmail and rape, thus on criminality. Unfortunately no one knows how often sexual intimacy is motivated by this type of pressure.

It is also coercion when one partner accuses the other of objecting to physical intimacy because of impotence or frigidity—an accusation that can impose a terrible pressure to perform.

Another common form of coercion must be mentioned: one partner threatens suicide if the other does not meet his or her sexual needs. Regrettably, manipulative behavior of this type is sometimes described as "love sickness."

Little need be said against coercion as the explanation or justification for intimate relations. Brutal selfishness is its own accusation.

To avoid becoming a victim of coercion, one must fight fear, flee from threats and resist pity. Those who give in out of pity, for example at the threat of suicide, surrender their independence and reward manipulative behavior. Threats prove lovelessness and selfishness, not tenderness and love. Anyone who uses such brutal methods should be denied success at any cost! Of course such a person also needs professional help, the care of a responsible and trustworthy psychologist or doctor.

The *fear of causing pain* is the fear of deeply hurting someone by saying a firm no. Even if a woman or a man knows that sexual intimacy is unwise, he or she often fears hurting or being hurt just the same. It is even more complicated when two partners have mixed feelings for one another: interest, but uncertainty and distance as well. Even two people who definitely like each other and know that their feeling is shared can hesitate and "beat around the bush" out of fear of causing pain to each other. Because they do not trust themselves to express their immediate feelings, they behave unnaturally. The effect this has on tenderness and sexuality is regrettable. Unwillingness to take a definite stand can cause people to go further in physical relations than they would really like to. In a relationship built on fear of causing pain, the partners tend to respond more strongly than their feelings and level of commitment warrant. When they later pause and reflect on their behavior, they become ashamed even to be together.

Fear of causing pain is not a sufficient ground for engaging in intimate relations, because it springs from emotional dependence. The partners in such a relationship are obviously not mature enough to stand up for their true feelings and beliefs.

Try Before You Buy

"Don't buy a pig in a poke" is an expression that comes from medieval marketplace customs. Unscrupulous merchants would put alley cats in gunny sacks, or "pokes," and then try to sell them as suckling pigs. Wise buyers did not put down cash until they had looked in the sack. (Sometimes this resulted in "letting the cat out of the bag"!)

"Don't buy a pig in a poke" sums up the argument of many who would like a free trial offer to find out if their partner is emotionally and, above all, physically compatible. Any possible subsequent disappointment should be prevented by this "materials testing." After a wedding it is too late for such a test, and the marriage may be doomed to fail. Fear of the possible failure of a marriage for sexual reasons is magnified by frequent published assertions that a marriage will succeed if "it works in bed."

Psychologist Ulrich Beer protests against trying sex out in his book *Love vs. Sex* (Tübingen: Katzmann-Verlag, 1967):

It is not possible to test a partner's suitability for marriage before the wedding. Sexual union outside marriage always occurs under circumstances that are completely different from those of marriage. The fear of pregnancy or just of being discovered, as well as the uncomfortable conditions in the back seat of a car, in the woods or on a couch, prevent the woman in particular from relaxing and make the act, or at least fulfillment and enjoyment, impossible. It is easy to fall into a sexual pattern in which the man quickly achieves orgasm while the woman rarely or never does. The result for the woman can be disappointment and a bad attitude toward sex; for the man it can be an outspoken and domineering attitude that makes courtship, tenderness and, above all, taking time appear superfluous. Finally, both suffer a very inhuman devaluation of the act of love, whose potential for joy and discovery they never experienced. In summary: Before marriage it is impossible to create experimentally the conditions that exist within marriage. [pp. 22-23]

People who advocate trying before buying may not understand

SEX BEFORE MARRIAGE: EVALUATING THE ARGUMENTS

the anatomy and function of the sex organs. Even the largest penis can penetrate deeply into a short vagina because the vagina is very elastic. To be sure, this elasticity depends very much on the woman's emotional state, on her degree of relaxation in the act of physical submission. This is exactly the requirement that is not met in a trial relationship! Those who ignore this fact necessarily draw the wrong conclusions from the results of their experiments.

It is a well-known fact that sexual behavior needs to be practiced. The experience of happily married people shows that it may take years for the necessary trust to grow. Only then is total emotional and physical devotion possible, with increasing creativity and joy in getting to know the body and feelings of one's partner and oneself.

To engage in sexual intercourse on a trial basis to avoid "buying a pig in a poke" is not only unloving, but an indication of ignorance as well.

People engage in premarital sexual intimacy for various reasons. Their needs, desires and fears are real and must be taken seriously. But many people do not realize that the instant gratification promoted by the sexual revolution actually works against establishing loving, tender, ultimately satisfying relationships.

It appears that sexual freedom is not a step forward, but a step backward in human development. It is striking that the progress of sexual liberation is paralleled by an increase in the divorce rate. Today's atmosphere of freedom increasingly ignores the importance of trust, love and responsibility, values that are prominent in the Christian message. We know from history what results when values are neglected. The moral decline of Rome was accompanied by the political decline of that world power.

Sexual freedom has not brought the expected great liberation; on the contrary, it has brought dependence and enslavement: to pleasure, to the pressure to perform sexually and to manifold fears. In spite of increased freedom and knowledge and an abundance of contraceptives, people are neither more satisfied nor happier than they were a generation ago.

If indeed the pursuit of sexual freedom has proved to be a step backward in personal and interpersonal development, then its harmful consequences must be evident. The next chapter will look at the harm that can result from sexual relations among young and unmarried people.

Warning— Danger Ahead

5

"Why don't you mind your own business?" someone might ask. "Let the lovers themselves decide what is right for them. What lovers do together should not concern anyone else!"

Of course this objection is valid. Love is a private matter, and I cannot interfere with anyone's personal responsibility and decisions. This is not what I want to do.

It is, however, the responsibility of every individual to alert others to danger where he or she has found that it exists. Danger is often not recognized by those who are exposed to it. This is the result not only of weak convictions, but also of lack of perspective. It is often difficult to see one's personal problems objectively.

In my work as a counselor and through many personal conversations, I have gained insight into the private lives of many people. Sexuality often plays a role in the pain I have seen, both in young people and in adults whose marriages are crumbling or destroyed. It is not my intention to impugn the seriousness of deep friendships. I am convinced that many couples firmly intend that "we two are going to do it right!" But we are all responsible for minimizing the risk of negative developments. To do this, we must know the dangers and avoid them: "An ounce of prevention is worth a pound of cure!"

The previous chapter was concerned with reasons for sexual intimacy. Let us turn from these theoretical arguments to concrete reality. Intimate premarital relations are risky. We can insure ourselves today against all kinds of accidents except in the area of intimate encounters. Since the only protection against emotional damage is personal responsibility, it is important to know any possible harmful consequences. From experience we know the following dangers: arrested emotional maturity, damaged relationships, epidemic selfishness, and destructive habits and memories.

Arrested Emotional Maturity

In my counseling practice I have repeatedly observed young people with little endurance, suffering greatly from boredom. I agree with those specialists who find the root of their unwillingness to make any effort, their dissatisfaction with life, in our consumer society and its constant emphasis on satisfying personal needs. Young people early in life are encouraged to demand whatever their childish hearts desire as well as to get to know the adult world: cigarettes, alcohol, automobiles and sexuality.

This head start on consumerism curbs boredom and avoids the tension that results from waiting. Continuous consumption makes it impossible to learn how to wait.

WARNING—DANGER AHEAD

But boredom and tension can lead to independent thinking, and only those people who have learned to wait can withstand stress and thus carry responsibility. Solid values and deep feelings, such as consideration, trust, tenderness and responsibility, require a long time to reach maturity. Maturation is possible only where there is a great investment of time and energy.

Everyone has experienced the difficulty of postponing strong sexual urges, of withstanding the tension. Many people think this is too difficult for them. They may rationalize at the first experience with petting or sexual intercourse that "once doesn't matter." But this is a grave error. The effect is often like the breaking of a dam: sexual desires can no longer be contained. The resulting "flood" may wash away modesty, self-respect and dignity. Standards for the selection of a partner, the situation and the type of encounter may be lowered, because "it doesn't matter anymore."

Perhaps someone will object that young people may enjoy sex now, become better adjusted in life later and still become useful members of society. But my concern is not with adaptation but with maturation. The extent to which maturation can be impeded and even prevented can be seen in the trial marriages that are so popular today.

At first the phrase *trial marriage* sounds promising. Two people who have slept together out of love for one another now provide themselves with the material security of a shared dwelling. They can live together as a married couple—but without the "superfluous marriage license"—and take their time finding out if they can really get along in everyday life. While they retain a great degree of freedom and independence, thus avoiding the risk of a premature commitment, their trial marriage also demonstrates a strong feeling of responsibility and the readiness to provide security. In theory, the trial marriage looks like the ideal solution, a most favorable arrangement that has benefit for everyone.

The reality is different. For John and Annette the expected freedom and independence became such an open relationship that in critical situations there was no sense of commitment. Basically they felt their relationship was temporary. The knowledge that either could still say no to the other inhibited the openness, depth and genuineness of feeling that is only possible in a stable marriage. Each was afraid of the tensions that could result from a direct expression of needs, expectations, criticism or fear.

Instead of maturing and solving conflicts, they learned to retreat and be silent. Fear—of causing hurt, of a possible resulting separation, of the subsequent loneliness—became more and more the reason for their continued life together. Without the final public decision for each other (marriage) both of them lacked security. The result was a superficial and artificially maintained togetherness that worked only when times were good, but bred feelings of suspicion and fear of desertion in crises.

For John and Annette, the price of trial marriage was high. The uncertainty and impermanence affected not only their emotions, but their plans for the future as well. As often happens in trial marriages, theirs could neither live nor die. Month by month and year by year they put off their decision about the possible marriage they were trying out, wasting precious time that could have been used to deepen their relationship. Instead of ascertaining whether or not they wanted to marry, they experienced increasing uncertainty and indecision. By living together they had become so used to each other that they were frightened by the thought of a possible separation. On the other hand, the unresolved problems of their uncommitted life together made the decision to marry seem unwise. And so John and Annette, frightened and uncertain, became ever more dependent on each other. They robbed themselves of chances for personality development and for planning for the future. Finally they developed feelings of dissatisfaction and inferiority which they expressed through aggression and depression.

Too late the couple finds out that while it is possible to rehearse a play, nothing of the kind is true of marriage. A trial marriage is a contradiction in terms. Just as it is impossible to try out living or dying, it is impossible to try out marriage! Even though there are seemingly happy couples who are just living together, it must be stated plainly: those who would enter a trial marriage are only trying to avoid a decision and are risking their own happiness and that of their partner.

This popular alternative lifestyle is directly related to the issue of premarital relations. No couple decides to live together without having first had intimate relations. Such relations are the first big step into an uncommitted relationship. Thus the harmful effects of trial marriage shed further light on the emotional damage caused by premarital sex.

Without the security of marriage, intimate relations can cause arrested maturity, and dependence takes the place of freedom and personal development.

Damaged Relationships
The arrested personal development in Annette and John's trial marriage in turn damaged their sexual relationship. It was greatly strained, even though their shared apartment offered them a certain security. The intimate contacts of young and unmarried people in insecure situations, in a car, in the woods or in their parents' house, are even more complicated.

Ted has finally managed to borrow his father's car. In a secluded part of the woods he has to find a certain plant for biology class—that was the reason he gave his father. Sylvia made a remark about visiting a girlfriend before leaving home and hurrying to meet Ted.

Both feel vaguely uncomfortable about lying to their parents, although they have been longing for this time of togetherness ever since they have realized that they are hopelessly in love. From the first passionate kiss they have felt irresistibly drawn together.

Ted knows of an out-of-the-way corner of the forest and stops on a well-hidden side road. Both are glowing with expectation and excitement. It helps them to forget the uncomfortable position in the car. Even applying contraceptive cream and putting on the condom bother them little. They discussed it all in advance. Sylvia does not want to take the Pill, and both want to be completely safe. So they agreed on this double protection.

Suddenly there is a noise and both of them jump. But soon their fear is forgotten in their need for physical closeness. It might be a long time before they have another opportunity this good. Because of their great longing for each other both of them even succeed in having an orgasm. Both are glad they have had this chance for physical intimacy.

On the way home, however, they become quiet and introspective. From minute to minute more questions come up to make them uneasy. Was it wrong to lie to our parents? What will we say if they ask about the plant or the girlfriend? What about this secrecy, this uneasiness, this time pressure, these preparations, this pressure to succeed? And what if we were observed? Are those unromantic contraceptives a good enough protection against pregnancy? There is always a chance that they won't work! A baby! That would really be terrible for everyone!

And then suddenly comes a disagreeable inner voice saying, "So what! Lots of girls get abortions!" Sylvia shudders. She never would have believed that she could have such thoughts. They will have to face a lot of fear until her next period! And what if it doesn't come? Sylvia begins to think about abortions and about someone who said he knew of a clinic if anyone needed one. What had they let themselves in for? Was it appropriate to their relationship for them to sleep together? Both are silently asking themselves, "What good did it do us? Was it worth the effort? What is going to happen now?"

It is no surprise that Ted and Sylvia begin to have the same two thoughts over and over again: "Why did I let myself go like that?"

WARNING—DANGER AHEAD

and "Why did he/she let this happen at all?" On the one hand we see self-criticism and guilt feelings, and on the other, blame that the partner did not take more responsibility for the relationship.

As important as the guilt question is the question of how both will deal with this shared experience. The relationship had been put under strain and made less certain by self-reproof and criticism of the partner. The best solution, to talk honestly about this experience and to lay clear ground rules for their future relationship, would be strenuous and difficult.

A different decision is more likely. Ted thinks the problem lies in their lack of experience, their uncertainty and clumsiness. He suggests a second rendezvous under better circumstances. He happens to know that Sylvia's parents are planning to drive to a meeting in two days. They can certainly count on being undisturbed in her parents' house for a couple of hours. Ted even apologizes for the awkwardness of the first time and begins to look forward enthusiastically to their next meeting. Certainly then everything will be more satisfying for both of them.

But Sylvia has grown hesitant and remorseful. She is now so ashamed that she wants to slap herself or sink into the ground. Just because of that one meeting she has risked her parents' trust. She is sad that sex has taken over so much of her relationship with Ted. Suddenly there is no more room for the wonderful tenderness and erotic tension that characterized earlier times together. Now somehow there is an emptiness between them. Their magical closeness has been sacrificed to their preoccupation with sex. Sylvia is disappointed with herself, but she is also disappointed with Ted: "Ted is older and more experienced than I am, and he should have known what he was getting me into." In the past she had found him fair and responsible, but now she begins to wonder. Is sexual satisfaction more important to Ted than caring?

Sylvia decides to break up with Ted.

Sexual relations between unmarried people are much more

susceptible to serious problems than are similar relations in marriage. The circumstances for intimacy between unmarried couples are much less favorable than they are for married couples. Instead of trust they learn mistrust, and instead of safety and security they experience uncertainty and fear. When things do not go right, disappointment and mistrust cause further misunderstanding between unmarried partners. In spite of the best intentions and the most intensive efforts, trust can be lost forever in the relationship.

The other possible result of premarital sex, that the couple will become preoccupied with sex, is also a danger to the partner relationship. The more sexuality moves into the foreground, the more conversation and the pursuit of shared hobbies are pushed aside. As sex becomes more important, there is less and less time and interest for getting to know the other person. The identity of one's partner eventually becomes unimportant. For the purpose of sexual satisfaction it does not matter if the partner is X, Y or Z. Loyalty is irrelevant to such a situation. Someone may say matter-of-factly that "at the moment" she is not going with X but with Y. Paradoxically, she calls the new relationship with Y "meaningful." It is a sellout of love and loyalty when people can be tossed aside like dirty shirts.

Epidemic Selfishness

Selfishness often characterizes the intimate relationships of unmarried people. Again and again women find that male friends quickly and emphatically begin to press for more intimacy and finally for petting and sexual union. From the age of puberty onward, men feel a strong sexual need. This often promotes the development of selfish attitudes and makes believable the old saw that "men are only after one thing."

In contrast to this male preoccupation, women are more likely to be reserved in matters concerning sexual satisfaction. This inclination to wait is true at least of those women who have not yet had sexual experiences. Strangely enough, many women still play the tempting but dangerous game leading to sex outside marriage, even if they clearly recognize that the man's intention is selfish. Why? Out of curiosity? Out of compliance or even submission?

Or is a woman's attitude toward the respective active and passive roles of men and women her reason for not wanting to risk saying no to a man's desire to possess? A woman's fear of rejection and loneliness is often covered up with common sayings: "That's what a man needs!" or "A real man is a conqueror and needs his freedom!" It is no surprise that some men take full advantage of this right to freedom so openly granted to them. The male dominance that so many women complain about has an important root here. If women have little self-respect, they will automatically be dominated by men. Female servility may also help to explain the existence of the crude jokes that circulate among men, jokes that deeply injure the dignity of women. On the same brutal level are the typical "manly" terms for sexual intimacy. It is pure selfishness to tell jokes or use expressions that degrade women, and to do so is to be guilty of emotional cruelty. Yet some men's selfishness is encouraged by women who play along or even just give in, for whatever reason.

Sexual egoism does not occur only in superficial relationships. It also exists in the most stable friendships. Steve and Kathy had known each other for several months. They had similar interests and liked to be together as often as possible. When they were alone they would tenderly hold hands or hold each other close, finding happiness in the warm embrace. Steve began to dream about touching Kathy under her clothing as well. The blood rushed to his head when he fantasized about petting and loving sexual union with her. He sensed also that Kathy's resistance was weakening. He finally took courage and whispered into her ear how much he would really like to be close to her. Her heart leaped with excitement because she had also begun to feel a longing for

Steve's body. But at the same time she felt strong hesitation and fear. She said that she would really rather wait.

Steve noticed her serious tone and that she had not by any means refused him. But at the same time he experienced negative feelings: disappointment, sadness, self-pity and finally anger toward Kathy, who in a way had left him "out in the cold." He became silent. Kathy's comment that she did not want to hurt him and had herself had similar desires for physical closeness did not help him out of his anger. Suddenly there was a gap in the formerly close relationship.

After a few days of uncertainty and distance, Kathy grew frightened. "Was I too hard on him? Maybe Steve is right and I am still too inhibited. Perhaps Steve just wanted to help me get rid of my silly inhibitions. I thought we were really in love—is it suddenly all over now?" In the meantime Steve was brooding, "Does Kathy really like me? If she does, then for my sake she ought to be able to give up her reservations. Maybe I should talk to her again."

Steve said to Kathy, "I have to know where I stand! It really frightens me to think that it could be over between us. You have to give me a sign. Kathy, if you still love me, then I want to sleep with you." After an inner struggle, Kathy gave in. Too late she found out that her sacrifice, made out of fear of losing Steve, had only rewarded his selfishness.

At this point several developments were possible. All of them would tend to reinforce Steve's selfishness.

Steve could stay with Kathy and continue to expect intimate sexual relations as proof of her affection. Kathy would have no more choice. Because she said yes the first time, she could no longer say no without risking the relationship that she bought so dearly with her first yes.

Steve might take Kathy's accommodation the wrong way, no longer seeing it as an indication of her love, but of her superficiality and lack of character. It sounds paradoxical to a woman, but a woman's no impresses a man, especially if he has put pressure on her in the first place. In many cases if the woman gives in, that only makes the relationship less secure! The man feels a silent disappointment and reproach at her quick submission.

It could even come to an open split. Steve might begin to look for a new girlfriend because the old one had lost her charm as a conquered woman. This would be an easy way out compared to the real solution: even after getting what he wanted, Steve could return to their original relationship and find new excitement in it if he would do his part, tenderly and responsibly, to deepen the friendship. Often men avoid this kind of effort. They find it more exciting to court a new girlfriend, especially since the first intimate contact has helped them get over some of their shyness. Guilt feelings can be easily pushed aside with the thought that the previous girlfriend was too "easy" and that this test had come at just the right time to be a warning against a serious relationship.

What does all this have to do with selfishness? The man's selfishness lies in the desire to possess. And the woman's selfishness? As strange as it may sound, the woman's selfishness lies in wanting to keep the man. Thus she also desires to possess. This type of selfishness will use anything to achieve its goals, even surrender in supposedly loving submission.

The potential for damage is obvious. Both run the risk that their sexual experience will reinforce their egotistical behavior and that they will continue to behave selfishly. Some men have gone so far in this direction that they rape their girlfriends. The man is at fault for never learning self-control and consideration, but the woman is also to blame if she encouraged his selfishness by giving in too early to his pressure for sex.

Selfishness also has a regrettable effect on the future course of events. Those who sleep together or engage in petting before marriage will probably not be willing to bear sexual tension after marriage—those times when, due to sickness or temporary separation, sexual contact is not possible and patience must be exercised. This inability to bear strain, so typical of selfish persons, can have a further effect. When a couple does not make the effort to find a solution to its problems and instead looks for a quick answer in sexual togetherness, they may develop a bad habit. Some couples try to solve all their problems in bed without paying attention to the causes.

If a person with selfish tendencies drops his or her partner after having sexual relations, it can also set a precedent for later relationships. If the person later marries, running away may mean committing adultery or getting a divorce. Psychologically speaking, this is what happens: avoiding the difficult task of solving a conflict brings temporary emotional relief. This pleasant feeling is its own reward, and behavior that is rewarded becomes more and more frequent. But there is danger in getting in the habit of running away from problems rather than solving them. Selfishness prevents the development of tenderness and responsibility toward a partner. Selfishness makes a person incapable of love, both before and in marriage.

Destructive Habits and Memories

The word *imprint* can help explain another danger of premature sexual union. To imprint a metal object means to make a lasting mark on it. Imprinting is also possible in human emotional development. Everything we experience makes an impression on us. These impressions influence our subsequent attitudes and behavior. A simple example is my reaction when a familiar telephone number is changed. Since the original number is imprinted on my memory, it usually takes a little while before I can dial the new number automatically.

Obviously the first sexual experiences make a strong impression —intimate relations always involve strong feelings. The more intense the feelings in the first sexual experience, the more future relationships will be affected by it. Apparently many young people do not wish to acknowledge this reality, but we must face the facts.

Every human being is especially excited at the time of his or her first experience with intimate relations. This excitement results from intense feelings such as joyful longing and burning curiosity or, on the other hand, humiliation, disappointment or even disgust. This experience marks the emotions the way the die marks metal. The impression made on the man is determined by the woman's behavior, as that made on the woman is determined by the man's. I want to emphasize that a strong impression is made on both partners, not on the woman alone! However, an anatomical imprint is made on the woman at the time of her first physical union—defloration, the rupture of the hymen.

Defloration usually results from penetration by the male sex organ. It can also occur when during petting a finger is inserted in the vagina. This is an important reason to take intensive petting seriously in a discussion of intimate relations.

Defloration is an imprint in the truest sense of the word. It is an irreversible occurrence. Because sexual intimacy and marriage used to belong together, English-speaking people have two expressions: *maid* and *matron*. This linguistic differentiation, which is much stronger in German and French, is based on an important perception: with her first physical union with a man, a girl becomes a woman. The imprint is usually not only physical, but emotional as well. Today many people question the importance of defloration. Perhaps they hope that "only once" is as good as "never." Without this wishful thinking, radical changes in sexual behavior would be necessary. For many people this thought is so unpleasant that they would rather convince their partners that "externals" don't matter.

But the so-called external resulting from the first physical union can make such a strong impression on the woman that she feels bound to the man. A young mother told me that she met her husband for the first time when she was thirteen years old. When she was fourteen and under the influence of alcohol, they had intercourse for the first time. From this time on she felt emotionally tied to him. If they had not eventually married, this first impression would have been a painful memory throughout all her later relationships.

Since the first experience with sexual intercourse makes such a strong impression, it will certainly set the tone for all subsequent experiences, whether with the same partner or with a different one. Let us first look at the harm that can result if the partner changes.

The new partner's personality will of course differ from that of the earlier partner. He or she has different habits, sexual habits in particular. I have emphasized that sexual impressions are strong because sexual needs and their satisfaction are accompanied by intense emotions. Thus the corresponding sexual behavior is also learned intensively, resulting in a firmly established sequence of motions that heighten sexual excitement. Previous sexual experiences bring habits and expectations into new relationships. This means that from the beginning it is necessary to learn new behavior and to adapt to new circumstances.

As habits developed with earlier partners are processed and adapted with each new partner, recollections and comparisons will naturally come to mind. Perhaps an earlier partner was more understanding, more active or more imaginative. Because it is impossible for all new experiences to be better than those that went before, unfavorable comparisons with the past will automatically be made. These memories not only disturb the one who has them; they make the new partner insecure as well.

An eighteen-year-old high-school girl who had never experienced sexual intimacy came to me for counseling. She explained sadly that everyday experiences with her boyfriend always brought

WARNING—DANGER AHEAD

similar experiences with her previous boyfriend to mind. Because she very much loved her current boyfriend, it depressed her to remember some of the especially beautiful times she had shared with the previous one. This sensitive girl was experiencing feelings that are even more likely to result from previous sexual relationships.

The first sexual experience lowers the threshold of resistance to sexual activity, thus weakening feelings of modesty. If the new partner is loved just as much as or more than the earlier one, then there is a spontaneous desire to share at least the same level of physical closeness with the new one. The new partner in turn expects to have at least the same "rights" as the previous partner. Those who dismiss such attitudes as petty underestimate the depth and breadth of our emotions.

The impressions made by sexual intimacy become downright dangerous when feelings of self-worth are hurt. The result can be guilt feelings—resulting from submitting too quickly and too early —or inferiority feelings. Both make it hard to find the courage to refuse subsequent sexual expectations. One cannot escape the thought that there is nothing left to lose.

There is always the possibility of openly discussing bothersome memories with the current partner. If these memories are conquered, the result may be even greater closeness. However, the risk of a crack or break in the relationship is great!

Even if a couple can cope with the excess emotional baggage, previous sexual impressions encumber the current relationship. Where emotional injury is great, it can be overcome only with considerable mutual effort.

Some may conclude that memories are a problem only if they are more beautiful than the present situation and thus cast a shadow on it. But this would be a misunderstanding. Even such a short thought as "with the other person things were different" can color a new relationship. Of great influence also are all the memories that arouse fear: remembered guilt or pain or rejection or disappointment. For a person with a history of sexual relationships, there are almost always memories of abused trust and violated modesty. All these memories are "on call." A similar experience can bring the past to life at any time.

Why take such a risk at all? Why let unnecessary sexual experiences darken the future? Is not the price paid for the immediate satisfaction of sexual needs much too high? And in case you are ready to engage in premature sexual relations not for the sake of your own needs but for those of your partner—is pity or consideration or even concern for the partner sufficient reason to encumber your own life?

Some readers may feel that the discussion so far has nothing to do with them personally. They have a responsible and stable intimate relationship with one partner and would not even think of changing. Besides, it is likely that they will marry their current partner. Given this, sex can do no harm.

There are no guarantees, however. No one can be completely sure that he or she will eventually marry and share the life of any particular partner. Too many things that do not matter today can play a decisive role tomorrow. Career and life goals are subject to change during the college years. One or the other may meet a third person who is even more attractive. Other, though admittedly less common, possibilities are serious chronic illness or an accident that cripples one partner. Each would create a totally new and completely unexpected situation.

A couple should together examine their attitudes to see if they are really ready to stay together in good times and bad. If they cannot affirm this, either they are not yet certain that they want to spend their lives together or they are not yet mature enough to make such a decision. If they are not mature enough for marriage, then they are not mature enough to assume the responsibility for an intimate relationship either.

Let us look at a case in which a couple eventually marries. This couple, let us say, abstains from physical union before marriage. Instead, they limit themselves to petting, during which both sometimes achieve orgasm. Is there any harm in this form of premarital intimacy?

Petting, like sexual intercourse, makes a strong impression. It can influence subsequent relations in marriage. If a man and woman have both become accustomed to petting as a means of achieving sexual satisfaction, then they have developed certain behavior patterns that bring the greatest satisfaction. Let us assume that they engage in sexual intercourse only after they are married. On the basis of their previous experience, they may find this physical union for a time to be not only strange but also unsatisfying. Both may be fixated at the level of the familiar and pleasant experience of petting, thus hindering the further development of the marriage relationship. There is another possible danger. Since the gentle touching that precedes sexual union normally includes petting, foreplay can trigger a defense mechanism by reminding the marriage partners of their premarriage practices, which are often associated with guilt.

Behavioral psychologists call this process classical conditioning. An originally neutral stimulus, the excitation of the sex organs, becomes closely associated with the guilt and fear that accompany premarital sex. Even in the best marriages these learned associations can come to life again at any time.

I encountered the following case of sexual maladjustment in my counseling practice. Sue and Jim had had frequent and intense sexual contact before marriage. They continued to enjoy and expand their sex life in marriage. But after a few years of marriage Sue began to resist sexual intimacy with her husband. Her reluctance grew into loathing. Both she and Jim were completely mystified and came for counseling. What had happened?

Only after a long delay had the damage become obvious. Even

though from the first both had fully affirmed the sexuality in their relationship, Sue had gradually begun to feel an inner reservation. She felt instinctively that the emotional side of their relationship was being shortchanged and that sexual contact could take place even in the absence of genuine love. She felt that sexuality had become pure sex and that as a person she did not matter. Personality was no longer important compared with sexual attraction. As Sue became aware of this she began to develop a loathing for herself and for her husband. Thus premarital sexual relationships, which so often take the place of developing emotional relationships, can be dangerous even if the couple later marries.

Even though it is obviously impossible to predict the future course of a relationship, it is possible to say with one hundred per cent certainty that people who accept this risk of premarital sex are playing not just with fire, but with their own happiness and that of their partner. When partners change, the happiness of a third and fourth person comes into play. These two people, as yet unknown, will also be encumbered by the excess emotional baggage of the premarital sexual relationship.

At this point some people might feel that the situation is hopeless. They have already been involved in an intimate relationship. Is marriage the only way to stop the spiral of damages? What if this partner is not the right one? Or what if there have been several partners?

No, in spite of all the difficulties that will need to be faced in a new relationship, the choice of a marriage partner should not be made under this emotional burden. It would be better to separate and make a good new beginning, better an end of horrors than horrors without end.

If some married couples can look back and say that they engaged in premarital sex and did not suffer any of the problems we have seen, it is still not a valid defense. The only possible response to this amazing assertion is, "Thank goodness!" One happy ending does not change the fact that the risk is great.

The more sexual experience one has, the more difficult it is to decide on a single life partner. The fear of marriage increases. Thus it is no coincidence that "living together" has come to be taken for granted.

In contrast to such temporary arrangements, actual marriage requires maturity, courage, emotional stability, decisiveness and responsibility, not to mention tenderness and love. One-sided sexuality inhibits or prevents the development of these qualities. Choosing to wait, on the other hand, can be a means of developing just those qualities needed for a happy future.

Choosing to Wait

6

Considering the many dangers of intimate relationships before marriage, some readers may have resigned themselves to making a virtue out of necessity. They see no choice but to struggle desperately to control their needs and fears and to try to convince themselves that patience and waiting can also be a good thing. But this does not really make anyone happy. Sober concepts such as "abstinence" or "chastity" do not sound the least inviting. I now face the honest question, "Learning patience is all well and good, but is it worth the effort? You're only young once and later on you won't be able to catch up on what you missed. You can't turn the clock back!"

It is important to consider the possible gain and loss of waiting. In weighing these two I believe waiting pays off! There are at least four benefits: emotional maturity, growth of tenderness, freedom of choice and a better society.

Emotional Maturity

I am convinced that everyone is capable of becoming emotionally mature. Everyone has gifts and abilities. However, the discovery of these treasures hidden in every person is complicated by premature sex. The decision to postpone sexual contact until marriage can be described as an exercise in self-control. But the old-fashioned concept of virtue is a better description. An etymological dictionary will show that the word *virtue* is derived from the Latin *virtus,* meaning strength, courage or moral excellence. While the word *virtue* may sound old-fashioned, the value it represents is timeless. A virtuous person is self-controlled, responsible, persevering, self-sufficient and independent. Virtue was obviously what a nineteen-year-old woman had in mind when she wrote, "If I marry at all it will only be when I am so strong and self-sufficient that I could make it on my own just the same."

There are other valuable qualities that are also necessary for emotional maturity: openness, genuineness, understanding and tenderness. To practice all these values is to learn to work, love and enjoy life. But too many people are willing to settle for only half the package.

Victor and Julie, for example, both are self-controlled, responsible, persevering, self-sufficient and independent. At least that is the way they see themselves. But they have proof too. While almost all the other young people flirt with one another, they have themselves completely in hand. They avoid parties of every kind. They are proud of themselves—but from the inside things look different. Both are inhibited and afraid of encounters with "the opposite sex," as they would say in their typically wooden manner. They suppress their erotic and sexual needs and hide behind a prudish and joyless life. They still hear the echo of parental admonitions: "That's dirty! You're not allowed to do that!" Victor and Julie are misapplying self-control to cover up their lack of emotional maturity. They are hard on themselves and make their lives narrow and poor.

It is completely different with Doris and Richard, who appear to specialize in the second-named group of characteristics. They enthusiastically flaunt their openness, genuineness, understanding and tenderness. They constantly take serious emotional risks. They openly express their deepest erotic and sexual needs and feelings. They hide their lack of emotional maturity by telling all and holding nothing back.

In contrast to these misunderstandings, emotional maturity involves awareness of oneself as a human being. It includes both the first set of characteristics, which emphasize *responsibility,* and the second, which emphasize *tenderness.* Both sets can be developed only with conscious effort. An external sign of the mature union of responsibility and tenderness is the willingness to wait until marriage.

This affirmation of waiting has nothing to do with the strained self-control of Victor and Julie, nor does it have anything to do with the distanceless superficiality of Doris and Richard. Instead, emotionally mature waiting accepts the tension between responsibility and tenderness. Fruit takes time to ripen. Those who are willing to wait long enough will harvest full, round and appetizing fruit. But those who experiment with it or pluck it too soon prevent it from growing and end up cheating themselves. An emotionally mature person is willing to wait, knowing that responsibility and tenderness do not develop overnight. Conversely, the act of waiting helps to develop the characteristics of maturity: self-control, responsibility, endurance, self-sufficiency and independence, openness, genuineness, understanding and tenderness.

Growth of Tenderness

One of the greatest benefits of saving sexual intimacy for marriage is the opportunity to discover and develop tenderness. Tenderness is one of the many ways of expressing love. It is closely related to Christian "brotherly love," which is a committed, giving love. Tenderness expresses intellectual and emotional closeness. Its focus is on *you,* the other person in the relationship.

In contrast to tenderness, "being in love" and "flirting" shift some of the focus back to *me.* Self-preoccupation is evident in the Greek concept *eros.* The words *erotic* and *eroticism* that often appear in film advertisements betray this preoccupation with "me" and "my" needs. At the same time the intellectual and emotional spheres lose ground to the physical.

This desire-love is clearly described by the Latin *sexus,* "physical sexuality." Sex, if it means only physical satisfaction, is diametrically opposed to tenderness. When one is concerned only with sexual satisfaction, the partner becomes simply an object of desire.

When eroticism is the principal component of sexuality, then love is truly blind. The lover becomes a means to satisfying a physical hunger, and his or her individual personality is lost sight of. In contrast, tenderness opens one's eyes to the beauty that is in one's partner simply because he or she is different. Tenderness has the freedom to enjoy the partner in everyday life.

Tenderness has an element of magic and mystery. As a blossom in a bud, it remains hidden from those who are impatient or possessive. But it reveals itself when it is honestly sought.

Nature gives us tenderness in many forms if we open our senses to perceive them. The word *tender* makes us think of touching, the contact of skin on skin. It reminds us of running barefoot by the ocean, the waves flowing around us, the sand of the beach warming us, the caress of the wind on our bodies. We find tenderness in the dew on the grass, fragrant blossoms and the songs of birds. When we experience tenderness we are aware of something important: we do not simply *have* bodies; rather we *are* bodies. That is why it is an attack on tenderness to neglect or hate our bodies.

Tenderness has both childlike and adult qualities. It has the curiosity and spontaneity of children and is sometimes downright playful. It has the objective sobriety of adults as well, as we can see in the responsible admonition and care given by loving parents.

Tenderness has many sisters. They are joy, warmth, trust, cordiality, happiness, security, responsibility, goodness, imagination, patience, hope, understanding, sympathy and openness.

Tenderness belongs in every life, because it is a human quality. It has many expressions, whether in word—a friendly remark, a happy song or a loving note—or action. We all have an almost limitless wealth of possibilities for expressing ourselves without words: a cordial and unpossessive handshake, a tender caress, a wave of the hand, a consoling touch, a meeting of the eyes, a happy wink, a flirting look or a mouth that tenderly smiles, nibbles and kisses. Music has endless possibilities for expressing tenderness. Pictures and special objects can be messengers of a tender love. A gift can bring a tender encounter to life, no matter whether it is valuable jewelry or only a pressed flower. Tenderness is also shown by carefully wrapping a present, attentively listening, preparing a tasty meal, opening a door, and a thousand other small, everyday things.

Often we do not know how wealthy we are. Tenderness enriches life for everyone, young and old, men and women, parents and children, the healthy and the sick. Without tenderness our lives would be boring and empty.

Responsible tenderness makes sexuality human. Otherwise the sex drive would overrun and destroy everything that is tender. No one is born with tenderness; it must be learned. Each phase of life gives opportunities to experience and practice tenderness: infants and small children in the relationship with their mother, children in the protection and security of the family, and young people in approaching a partner. People who love each other should not keep their distance. They must learn to approach each other with tenderness and without being possessive. Tenderness is a lifelong concern, a continual struggle with selfishness. It takes a long time for people who love each other to mature in tenderness. They should give themselves time.

Tenderness has nothing to do with cheap sentimentality. It is not a utopian dream but a typically human need. We all search and long for tenderness because it is necessary in our lives. Where there is tenderness there is no room for uncertainty, fear and mistrust. With tenderness come security and trust, which are necessary for a healthy life.

Opportunities to love and grow are certainly not without danger. Fearing the abuse of tenderness through premarital intimacy, some people end up fearing tenderness itself. Others carry tenderness to tiresome extremes.

Andrea knows the disadvantages of premarital relations. Thus she avoids everything that might awaken emotions in herself or her boyfriend. She labels their type of relationship platonic love and is proud that "absolutely nothing has happened" between them. This misunderstanding of tenderness must be exposed as emotional brutality, whether this strained relationship was born out of a noble but twisted understanding of love or out of inhibitions, genuine fear of contact with the opposite sex.

Jeff, by contrast, is so enthusiastic about tenderness that he continually wears his heart on his sleeve. He communicates these feelings to everyone he likes, not only in words, but also in continual attentiveness. After a while even his girlfriend feels as if she is being smothered.

Tenderness gives the opportunity to learn something essential about life and about interpersonal relations as well. In general only those people who are willing to accept and master the natural tension in love will find the hidden treasure, tenderness. Such mastery brings profit without any loss and allows full freedom in the later choice of a partner.

Freedom of Choice
We have investigated the consequences of premarital sexual intimacy and we have seen the expected freedom reveal itself as enslavement. Premature sex shifts people onto the wrong track. The sex drive is so strong and the impression made by petting and intercourse is so great that sexual contact soon acquires undue importance in the relationship. Thus tenderness and responsibility are automatically pushed aside. The sexual desire to possess steals one's own freedom as well as that of the partner.

Of course abstinence will not alone make one free. Ronald and Evie, an established couple, emphasize freedom in their relationship, but they carry it to extremes. Often when they are together they stress their self-sufficiency and independence. They are proud that they can tolerate any sort of freedom in their relationship—dating others, not discussing important personal matters and, of course, independently pursuing hobbies and interests without considering the other's plans. They do not know that this is a caricature of a relationship. What they have is not freedom but lack of commitment.

Mary and Tom also misunderstand freedom. Because they want to remain independent, their relationship has become strained. They continually force themselves to stay distant from each other and to act liberated even though it is not at all what they want. All their talk of freedom produces nothing but torment and anguish.

What do we gain if we consciously practice tenderness instead of independence and distance on the one hand, or sexual contact on the other? The immediate benefit is freedom, with other advantages in the future. Tenderness allows both partners to feel comfortable and independent in their relationship, but in no way uncommitted. Without physical union, they are naturally spared the fear of unwanted pregnancy. The availability of effective contraceptives may make this fear less evident, but it is present in the subconscious just the same. Undoubtedly the best "method" of contraception is responsibly waiting until marriage. Only in this way is it possible to feel free, free of fear and free to see the future in perspective.

Only those who have allowed each other to remain free by refusing to engage in petting and sexual intercourse before marriage can freely decide to spend their lives together. Obviously, such a freely made decision is much more reliable than the "sex test," the supposed test of compatibility. The decision to marry is so important that it must be made free from all pressure—whether the pressure results from a desire to make things right (because of previous sexual intimacy) or from the expectations of other people or from having a child on the way. Tragically, couples often begin a marriage under this type of pressure—not freely at all.

Many, it seems, have no interest in the freedom I have praised so highly. They even consciously forgo their right to freedom and instead live for their sexual needs. Such people may have a simple philosophy of life: "The only thing that matters is what I have right now!" In other words: "What I have right now, the opportunity for sexual intimacy, is more important to me than the institution of marriage. For many people marriage only brings unhappiness anyway. For most people a happy marriage is to be found only in the imagination or in fairy tales. Why should I give up premarital sex?"

We can all understand this attitude. It results from disappointment and resignation. Preparing for the future seems unimportant because marriage has lost its appeal. Here we have one of the tragedies of our society. Too few people conduct their marriages in a way that appears attractive and exciting to others.

A Better Society

Our society suffers from a lack of good examples. Some observers have spoken of "the fatherless society." We could expand this and speak of the motherless and "familyless" society as well. The large number of single-parent families, the exploding divorce rate and the increasing isolation of old and sick people reflect a society without commitment. There are few exciting marriages and families. For many people marriage means shackles, confinement, boredom and the loss of individual freedom. It seems to have become a prison.

A nineteen-year-old woman from an unbroken home described her view of marriage: "I personally am afraid of marriage, simply because I have almost never seen a happy one. Just the thought of being bound to someone for the rest of my life frightens me. So I have promised myself that I will never let anyone push me around. Marriage means less and less to people my age. And when I see how married couples lose their individuality and steal each other's freedom, and how even single people are automatically isolated by the institution of marriage, I don't think it is at all bad that the idea of marriage is losing ground."

Our society lacks not only tender and loving married couples, but also attractive models of how young people can treat each other openly and affectionately without being caught in a sexual relationship.

One symptom of this situation is that hardly anyone knows what an engagement is for. It has lost its original meaning: the public commitment of two partners to one another. Only adults can make this commitment, not boys and girls in their early teens and certainly not children! And yet we all know of serious relationships between early teen-agers that have in their sexual intensity long since gone beyond what is appropriate for engagement and that more closely resemble marriage.

Compare the development from acquaintanceship to friendship, to engagement and finally to marriage, with the construction of a house. Sexual union after marriage could be the roof of the house. A one-sided emphasis on sexuality would mean that the roof would stand alone, without walls or foundation. I fear that more and more homes are being built "in thin air" without the foundation of responsible and loving tenderness. In our society we have become so accustomed to marriages without foundations that they appear normal to us. As a result, few are alarmed when young people substitute erotic experiences for the development of emotional maturity. I even know parents who encourage young people in sexual promiscuity—that is how sick our society has become!

Since attractive examples of marriages and families are hard to find, many people are looking for alternate lifestyles to replace the institution of marriage, which looks old-fashioned and sick. Unmarried couples who live together are common. The more adventurous may recommend mate-swapping or even group marriage. A social worker in an administrative position, married and the father of several children, started a relationship with a female colleague who then became pregnant. He brought the girlfriend and their child into his family and lived with two women and their children. It is hard to imagine how this composite family could successfully deal with the emotional strain of such a web of relationships. Polygamy does not even work in countries that are quite used to it, an African marriage counselor assured me.

Our uncommitted society desperately needs help to overcome this hopeless confusion about how to build solid marriages. Professionals such as social workers, doctors, pastors, counselors and psychologists can give plausible answers only when they have solved these problems in their own private lives. Yet the job of healing our sick society is much too big for the few qualified experts to handle alone. It is a job for all of us.

But can an individual really make a difference? In my opinion, certainly! We all can become good examples for those in our lives. To be an example means neither missionary fanaticism nor pharisaical hypocrisy, but the courage to go one's own way, standing alone if necessary, in the search for tenderness. Since we all are in contact with many other people every day, the snowball effect is possible. An avalanche of people could once again say yes to life by putting tenderness and responsibility before the simple satisfaction of sexual needs. People could again find hope and radiate it to those around them. But making a difference will be possible only for those people who can free themselves from the tyranny of needs or of peer pressure. Is this an unrealistic dream? No! Everyone has the opportunity to be an influence, perhaps not in a big way with a lot of sacrifice and show, but quietly in everyday life. We can all commit ourselves, wherever we may be, to making our lives more humane, particularly where sexuality is concerned.

As a counselor it hurts me to meet young people who risk their happiness by becoming too intimate too early in their relationships. In addition to the emotional damage we have already discussed, there are wrecked marriages that would not have been started except for a premarital sexual relationship. These marriages have led to scrapped educational plans and unwanted children who may suffer for the rest of their lives. Those who engage in or approve of premarital sex not only risk their personal happiness, but work to quench new hope for our society.

It may be that after an honest and critical self-examination, some people who have engaged in premarital sex will find no sign of damage in their personal development. Such people are just plain lucky. But still, harm has been done, because they let the opportunity slip by to provide a good example for society in its search for tenderness. They have, in fact, become counter-examples, models for all those who would prefer to satisfy their needs immediately rather than strive for emotional maturity. Going one step further, we could say that they are guilty of unintentional seduction: they lead people to take a risk that has ended in tragedy for so many. Someone who accomplishes the amazing feat of learning to swim simply by jumping into the water could cause the unhappiness of many other people. Most of the people following that example would not swim but sink. The risk of following an atypical example is simply too great!

Earlier I mentioned the graduating kindergarten teachers. Fifteen of the twenty unmarried women wanted to live with their boyfriends without getting married. When I stop to think that these women were trained to teach children and help them form attitudes about life, it frightens me. What examples of marriages and families our children are being exposed to! Adultery and divorce are common among people in all social and educational professions—social workers, teachers, marriage and family counselors, psychotherapists, psychologists and even pastors.

Our society desperately needs healthy marriages and families, and the path toward these is set in childhood. Tragically, the choice between the attractive offer of the sexual revolution and the opportunity to develop tenderness and responsibility is often made early. Between the ages of twelve and seventeen the die may be cast. But young adults do not need to be controlled by their past. They can re-evaluate the evidence for and against premarital sexual intimacy.

Taking Stock
7

The sexual revolution offers personality development through uninhibited sexual satisfaction. The way of tenderness offers the true development of a creative and original personality, complete personhood rather than mere sensuality.

The sexual revolution offers a more intense experience of the partner relationship through petting and sexual intimacy. The way of tenderness offers a loving and realistic experience of that relationship.

The sexual revolution offers a supposedly risk-free method for deciding on a marriage partner by testing sexual compatibility. The way of tenderness offers true freedom of choice for the simple reason that there is no physical commitment.

The sexual revolution offers a way to keep up with the times by getting rid of old taboos. The way of tenderness offers responsible thinking for the present time instead of merely swimming with the current.

The tables have turned. The one who was laughed at because of his or her chastity before marriage is no longer the supposed loser, but the big winner. Such people can experience the true joy of life! They have opportunities to learn emotional maturity, to discover tenderness, to gain true freedom in choosing a marriage partner, and to make a responsible contribution to society.

Now the "natural" and "progressive" advocacy of premarital sex must give way to the question, "Why run such a great risk only because someone is no longer willing to wait?" The answer is obvious. Those who wish to enjoy sexual intimacy without the security and protection of marriage are reckless and irresponsible—to themselves, to their partners and to society.

It is not easy to assert that forgoing premarital relations pays off, particularly in a society that takes them for granted. Whenever I recommend choosing to wait, I know that my hearers may be having a variety of reactions ranging from hostility to disbelief. Before looking at the many rewards of tenderness, let's pause to evaluate several possible reactions to the idea of premarital chastity.

Pat Me on the Back
Some readers have probably reacted with joy, with thankfulness for being preserved from harm, or with satisfaction at finding confirmation of their own value of responsible behavior. Of course I am pleased when people like what I have to say, but I must give this warning: sometimes agreement can become self-satisfied moralizing or even gloating. This change comes from a hypocritical attitude: how bad everyone else is in comparison with oneself. Moralists draw their strength from misunderstanding sexuality on

the one hand and responsible tenderness on the other.

Fidelity Is Only for Your Wife

The "double standard" is a common attitude—behavior that I accept for myself I reject for my partner. A person who lives by the double standard typically alternates between strong emotions, jumping back and forth between smugness and indignation depending on whether he happens to be in the position of winner or loser.

A winner is a person who benefits from the double standard. Although involved in a serious relationship, on the side he has another sexual contact. He protests smugly to his partner that there is nothing wrong with the situation and even speaks in terms of love and personal development and freedom. For the most disloyal behavior he has such a good explanation that it is all supposed to sound noble, helpful and good. And then it happens! Unexpectedly the tables are turned; his partner has in turn found another sexual contact. Suddenly the winner has become a loser, and just as suddenly he becomes an expert on propriety and morality! What he earlier called "progressive" and "normal" he now calls by its right name again: selfish, disloyal and heartless. His ideas on morality differ enormously, depending on the situation.

This double standard can also have a regrettable effect in the area of sex education. Unfortunately, many parents and teachers still give different advice to boys and girls on the subject of sexual contact. "A man has much more sexual freedom than a woman," they say or imply. "Young men must sow their wild oats." Because our society is still very male-oriented, the man automatically benefits from the double standard. This attitude is clearly selfish. Many men who hold it nevertheless expect one day to marry a virgin. One can only wonder what happens to all the female "guinea pigs" with whom the young men have gathered their experience.

The double standard is terribly brutal and inhuman! When, due to a misunderstanding of liberation, a woman becomes sexually active outside of a serious relationship, a man takes offense because one of his supposed rights is threatened. What the man smugly enjoyed, he will attack with moral arguments if he is the loser.

Parents may also hold the double standard. If their son is gathering experience with girls, they are winners. But if their daughter has a sexual relationship with another family's son, it is quite a different matter. Suddenly the "gentlemanly indiscretion" or "small slip" becomes an "irresponsible seduction" or even "rape."

Marriage Does Not Mean Security

Another possible reaction to the idea of premarital chastity could come from people who are in serious relationships or even living with someone. They might say that a marriage license is not necessary for security and safety. Without questioning the genuineness and seriousness of such relationships, I remain firmly convinced that there can be such trials for a couple that at times the only thing that holds them together is the marriage license. The license may even be a painful reminder of the vows. Even if such a crisis should continue for months, this decision made before witnesses gives the couple an opportunity to pull itself together. The knowledge that one's spouse, if only for legal reasons, cannot simply decide to leave provides a sense of security and protection which cannot be underestimated. This sense continues to influence the emotions subconsciously even if all the conscious feelings favor separation or divorce.

This answer may not satisfy someone who is unhappily married and is angry over the prison created by the institution. We understand only too well when he or she laughs bitterly at the mention of the security of marriage. Yet this is a tragic misunderstanding.

Marriage gives every opportunity for an ideal sharing of two lives. This is the topic of the next chapter, where I will deal with the purpose of this book—developing the capacity for loving marriages and families.

Chastity Is for Fanatics

In the meantime, many readers are probably feeling angry about our discussion of premarital chastity. My no to premarital sexual relationships and yes to waiting and emotional maturity may strike them as narrowminded, naive or antisexual.

Others, who have followed my train of thought, will accept the logical and psychological basis of my arguments. But these people also may experience anger over my "simplistic" conclusion. They may feel that any one-sided answer is simply too extreme and for that reason alone can be only part of the truth. Does not the truth usually lie in the middle? A compromise should be possible. The answer must be neither a total affirmation nor denial of intimate relationships, but rather a subtle differentiation: who can have premarital sexual contact with whom and under which circumstances? This is the only way to do justice to all points of view. One could curb the excesses of the sexual revolution and at the same time retain some of its benefits in terms of liberation from prudish antisexual attitudes.

At first this sounded correct to me too. For years I searched for the "golden mean." Everything in me resisted dogmatic answers. I wanted to argue with Christian pronouncements on the subject of sex before marriage. Waiting in order to achieve emotional maturity seemed unnatural and inhuman to me in its hard consistency. But I must insist that my one-sided and thus annoying conclusion is based on verifiable facts. I remain convinced that it is valid, even though some of my colleagues and even liberal theologians hold opposing views.

An angry person can refuse to accept my conclusion that sexual intimacy must be protected by marriage, but even a person who takes my conclusion seriously may experience sadness or fear: sadness over the past or fear for the future.

I remember many beautiful hours I spent getting to know my wife: the wonderful erotic tension and the daring advances. The mixture of fear and desire excited me greatly. But I also remember the feeling of shame at having gone too far. Sometimes the original excitement and expectation disappeared entirely, replaced by disappointment with myself or with her. We did not have physical union until after we were married, but in retrospect we believe we still made many mistakes. We sometimes paid too little attention to the faint feelings of uneasiness that could have warned us of coming sadness and disappointment. My own experiences have made me sensitive to the needs of many unmarried people.

It's Too Late for Me
Many people feel sadness over the past. They may have entered a sexual relationship because of misguided fears or desires. Perhaps they recognize the damage or the missed opportunities. Perhaps they are so disappointed with themselves or with the partner that their sadness borders on defeat. No matter how a person's past may look, he or she always has the opportunity to replace old attitudes and behavior patterns with new ones, though it may require much effort. It is possible to rebuild from ruins if one has the courage and strength to clear aside the rubble. An unfortunate past can be overcome! Christians even may, through forgiveness, make a completely new start.

Others may be sad because they have waited and waited with iron discipline and now see that out of fearfulness and inhibitions they have ignored the need for tenderness and love. Here too it is possible to make decisive changes in direction.

In contrast to sadness over past actions, fear is concerned with the future. "All that about the emotional damage of premature sex and the benefits of practicing tenderness sounds reasonable," someone may say. "But how can anyone live like that? A person with a normal, natural sex drive will certainly be overstrained. After all, to stop short of petting shows no small degree of self-control!" I know from experience, however, that even today unmarried people need not be overtaxed when they have a serious relationship but do not sleep together. I know a number of married couples who waited until after marriage—without becoming inhibited or suffering other harm.

Others may worry that whatever they do will turn out wrong. "You warn against taking sexuality too far in a relationship," they may protest. "But at the same time you warn against too little, against an inhibited, antisexual attitude! How can a person know what to do?" This question must be answered in actual practice as one tries to find tenderness, the happy medium between sex and prudery. Later we will look closely at the possibilities for practicing tenderness, but let us now look at the rewards of tenderness.

The Rewards of Tenderness
8

Whether we marry or not, we need love to survive. We all need to receive love as well as to give it.

In spite of the high divorce rate, in spite of bad experiences with partners, parents or friends, and in spite of the convenient alternative of "living together," most people still strive to find and give love through marriage. Perhaps one reason is that many people no longer see marriage as a commitment "till death us do part." More and more people see marriage as an impermanent contractual arrangement. For the most part, this is due to increasing indifference and resistance to spiritual matters and particularly to God. The changes in divorce laws have also made their contribution. So-called incompatibility, a flexible concept, is now a sufficient reason for divorce in most states.

Strong Marriages
Instead of a temporary contractual arrangement, I understand marriage to be a decision for lifelong commitment. Many people marry for entirely the wrong reasons: to increase social status, to get away from parents, as a prerequisite for having children, as insurance against material want or loneliness or sickness or old age, or as a passport to sexual fulfillment. Relationships founded for these reasons are alliances based on need, but they have nothing to do with the real purpose of marriage! For me, the wedding represents neither the long-awaited Christmas morning nor the beginning of lifelong imprisonment.

This is a picture of marriage as I understand it: a tender, loving and mature man and woman begin a highly adventurous, exciting and sometimes demanding journey together, with all of its risks and opportunities. Their journey has great promise, at least at the beginning, because of their unity of spirit and love for one another. It is completely up to them which parts of their trip to share and which to go alone. They alone are responsible for how fast they go, for the direction they take, for stops and above all for the traveling conditions they create.

There are rules of the road, nonetheless. They must learn to understand and be understood, to give and take, and above all to accept each other—differences and all. These rules must be learned and practiced together, which will always cause friction. But crisis situations give an opportunity to prove that this little team we call marriage has learned to solve problems together. No one has to bail out in case of difficulty, not even in the worst case, adultery, when at first everything seems to be lost. Even in this catastrophic situation it is possible to ask for and receive forgiveness. Then it is once again possible for both partners to devote all their energy to making the stranded marriage seaworthy again.

In happy marriages two people share their lives and future through thick and thin. Trust and self-protection, closeness and distance, accommodation and individuality, and freedom and commitment can all be developed in such a marriage. These pairs of opposites, or "poles," do not face each other as hostile brothers but as equal partners that complement each other. Marriage allows an ever more lively exchange between two such poles, promoting a healthy tension between them.

Of special importance is the tension between the poles *I* and *you,* between self-realization and self-sacrifice. The complementary nature of these two poles and the corrective exchange between them is what gives life to both partners and the marriage. When one pole, for example self-realization, predominates, the result is imbalance and eventually breakdown. Without the corrective influence of self-sacrifice, self-realization becomes pure selfishness. On the other hand, self-sacrifice is dangerous if there is no self-protection. Self-sacrifice would soon become self-surrender. The strength of one pole suddenly becomes weakness when its opposite pole does not balance it.

Perhaps marriage as I have described it sounds too good to be true. For this reason I will not stop with a mere description of a strong marriage. I will describe the way to achieve it as well.

Responsible Loving

Practical questions deserve careful answers. How can people learn to practice tenderness and responsibility? Here are some realistic answers to the many questions that have come my way.

People who want to practice tenderness must (1) recognize tenderness and responsibility as necessary guidelines, (2) affirm sexuality—but in harmony with tenderness and responsibility, (3) accept themselves, and (4) accept general ethical principles.

The first prerequisite, recognizing tenderness and responsibility as guidelines, is anything but obvious. Present-day sources of wisdom in questions of love and sexuality are statistically-oriented sexologists and the consumer society with its need-satisfaction ideology. To learn tenderness and responsibility, we need more reliable leaders. These leaders can be tenderness and responsibility themselves if we incorporate them into our behavior. Tenderness and responsibility are poles that are in tension with each other and that complement each other. Only when both work at the same time can "desiring love" develop into "giving love."

The second prerequisite emphasizes the natural meaning of sexuality, but at the same time opposes any one-sided development in the direction of the sexual revolution. It means that certain attitudes must be abandoned, such as that it is normal for young and unmarried people to have experience in petting or sexual intercourse, or that a man must gather sexual experience before he marries. Instead, sexuality should be allowed to develop, protected by and in harmony with tenderness and responsibility. Sexuality and tenderness are not opposites; sexuality is not the enemy of love.

The challenge of the third prerequisite is ably presented in the book *Love Yourself* by Walter Trobisch, marriage counselor and author. At first glance self-acceptance seems to have nothing to do with longing for tenderness. The challenge to love yourself sounds almost like the motto of an egotist. But this call has the same content as God's basic command in both the Old and the New Testaments: "You shall love your neighbor as yourself" (Lev 19:18; Mt 22:39; Mk 12:31; Lk 10:27).

In modern terms this self-love means that I accept myself. But have I fully and completely accepted myself? My abilities? My limitations? My weaknesses? Have I accepted my lot in life? My sex? My sexuality? My age? Can I affirm my financial situation? My health? My appearance? In short: Do I love myself? Only those who love themselves can love their neighbors as well.

Self-acceptance is related to emotional maturity and independence. Emotionally unstable people often seek support from their partners to compensate for their own instability, but it is dangerous to use partnership and marriage to make up for emotional immaturity!

The fourth prerequisite is vital. Do I accept ethical principles as they are found in philosophy, in the Bible and in folk wisdom? In philosophy we have the "categorical imperative" of Immanuel Kant: "Act in such a way that your principle of action could safely be made a law for the whole world." Much earlier, Jesus taught the same wisdom with simpler words: "Whatever you wish that men should do to you, do so to them" (Mt 7:12). This has been popularized as the golden rule: "Do unto others as you would have them do unto you." If we apply this principle to sexuality, no more double standards of any kind are possible.

Balanced Relationships

We must avoid two misunderstandings of tenderness and responsibility: a one-sided tenderness without the protection of responsibility, and a one-sided responsibility without the protection of tenderness.

Tenderness without responsibility is simply sex in disguise. With some couples it takes the following form: they draw the line at sexual intercourse and intensive petting, but up to that point they irresponsibly play with fire. A supposedly progressive psychological clinic strongly encourages all kinds of physical contact short of sexual intercourse. Such a practice of "tenderness" does indeed help reduce inhibitions and compensate for sexual inexperience, but inhibitions are replaced by their opposite extreme, license and shamelessness. True tenderness and responsibility are lost as well. This dead end torments the couple because sexual experiments up to a certain boundary naturally arouse both partners without satisfying their pent-up needs.

Responsibility without tenderness is the second misunderstanding. An extreme interpretation of responsibility results in brutal coldness. This happens when two people with an exaggerated feeling of responsibility and a fear of sexuality take care not to come close to one another. When they walk together they stay at a safe distance, and when they talk they avoid eye contact. A friend told me about a couple like this. "Dirk tries every way he can to make his girlfriend adopt his cold, arrogant manner because she supposedly needs it to live with him. This training in toughness is slowly but surely turning her into an emotional wreck. She never hears an encouraging word from him. He never praises her at all. That is part of the training." But if tenderness is excluded, pure responsibility robs people of their humanity!

There is also a third dead end which coolly avoids both tenderness and responsibility. Some young people find it completely normal for both sexes to share the same tent while camping, to sleep in the same room or even to share the same bed without actually "sleeping together." I have counseled a thirteen-year-old girl who spent the night in the same sleeping bag with a boy. On the outside she acted very casual, saying there was nothing to it. But I wonder about the hidden emotional strain for people who put their natural desires "on ice." And I wonder how much energy must be devoted to self-deception and dishonesty toward those around them when "being cool" does not work! This is one way to unlearn tenderness and responsibility.

How can one learn to practice tenderness and responsibility? Andy, Marian and Tina illustrate the pitfalls to avoid and the problems to overcome.

Andy does not have a girlfriend. This bothers him a lot. It especially hurts when he sees almost all his friends with serious friendships.

It is important for Andy to free himself from peer pressure, whether he has actually been the object of ridicule or if he only fears it. He must neither panic at the thought that time is running out nor retreat to his own four walls. Instead he should lay the groundwork for getting to know someone with whom he could form a friendship.

The conditions for forming relaxed and casual friendships and also for practicing tenderness and responsibility are especially good when young people spend time together in a mixed group. Best of all are the youth groups that meet in many churches. They usually offer a variety of activities that appeal to a wide range of talents and interests. On the other hand, some young people prefer special-interest groups such as sports teams, ski clubs or the school band. A planned schedule and the presence of leaders automatically protects against boredom.

Boredom motivates more and more young people to get out of the house to see whom they can meet. Then they stand around somewhere with others or go to bars or video arcades. These chance meetings of bored people would probably soon lose all appeal if it were not for a few inexhaustible topics: sex, alcohol and possibly drugs. At these meetings the older ones naturally swap stories. It does not matter how much of what they say is actually true—their adventures sound exciting and desirable. Slowly but surely the values of the inexperienced newcomers are influenced and pressed into a new mold.

Much of the misinformation young people hear on the streets could be cleared up in an honest discussion with their parents, but unfortunately these discussions are rare after puberty. Besides, some popular magazines give such great emphasis to young people's independence and need-satisfaction that they are encouraged, sometimes even directly, to disobey their parents. Given such influences, it is no surprise that some young people and even children are becoming more radical. In my counseling practice I have met twelve-year-olds who have declared complete emotional independence from their parents and who move in circles where recreation consists of sex, smoking and drinking. It is alarming how unchildlike and impoverished is the world of many ten-to-fourteen-year-olds. This is most often the case where their parents' marriage is unhappy and the entire family atmosphere is full of tension. Disturbed families seriously threaten the development of the children.

To return to Andy—when he someday decides that he would like to get to know someone better, then he should ask himself some important questions: "What is my real reason for wanting to get to know this person? Is it my longing for tenderness, or only sexual curiosity and a desire to possess?" The following question is also important: "Am I looking for a casual friendship or a serious involvement?"

As the relationship grows more personal the question arises, "Can I picture this person as a lifelong friend or marriage partner?" If the answer is no, then it would be reckless, unfair and irresponsible to take further steps.

According to the guidelines of tenderness and responsibility, more questions become important when one begins to take a special interest in one person. "Am I ready for the possibility that we may be together for a long time or perhaps for the rest of our lives? Are we old enough to get seriously involved with each other? What are our plans for the future, especially concerning education? How independent are we of our parents, emotionally and financially? What do our parents think of a serious friendship? What is my friend's family like? Will they put too much strain on our relationship? Could it result in serious conflicts?" It is an unavoidable fact that one does not simply marry a person, but marries into a family. This can cause a lot of pain when the partner one loves comes from a family one cannot stand. And finally, "Is the time right for a serious relationship?" An early emotional attachment only lengthens the already difficult wait until marriage.

In contrast to the lonely Andy, Marian seems to be doing well.

THE REWARDS OF TENDERNESS

She is not in a special-interest club or youth group, but in a clique of young people between the ages of twelve and eighteen. They are not delinquents although sometimes they really raise the roof. They like to meet in homes where the parents are absent so they will not be disturbed. They listen to records and smoke and dance and drink (someone always brings something). And they have fun! Their games are exciting—"forfeits" or "spin the bottle" with kissing or even undressing. So many want to come to their parties that now no new people are allowed, except maybe pretty girls.

To some people this all sounds quite harmless. They are used to worse things. But conditions such as these slow the development of tenderness and responsibility. These gatherings are the first steps down the path leading to a disinclination to work, manifested in truancy or changing jobs frequently or unemployment, and above all to a one-sided emphasis on sex instead of tenderness and love. Besides, this situation is ideal for creating nicotine, alcohol and drug dependencies.

It is likely that most newcomers to such a group have mixed feelings. At least at first, they vacillate between curiosity and resistance. The danger is great that the older and more experienced members will try to explain away their hesitation as immaturity and inhibition. The resulting emotional confusion is expressed well in a cry for help I found in a letter published in a young people's magazine: "I am a fourteen-year-old girl and am afraid of parties. They always play games like 'spin the bottle,' games where you have to kiss boys. I feel like I have to play along, but I don't know how to kiss. When a boy wants to give me a French kiss, I just can't —even when I like the boy. I get so embarrassed that I'm afraid of every party. My question is, Are there certain rules for French kissing? How should a girl behave?"

Obviously this girl feels pressured to conform to the rules and norms that "everyone" observes in such situations. Out of curiosity or fear of rejection, she does not heed her emotional resistance. She continues to go to the parties. Her hesitation shows itself in her fear of being embarrassed. The danger is that this girl will finally conform, contrary to her true feelings.

In these situations one can only hope that young people will recognize their freedom of choice and use it. They can learn to remain true to their own feelings, not allowing themselves to be unduly influenced by others. Young people too can take responsibility and speak up when party games or other group activities do not appeal to them.

Some young people have a "lifeline" at home—their parents. But this presupposes a good relationship. The parents must know where their children are, whom they are meeting, and how they are spending their free time. Tragically, some parents are either extremely naive or irresponsibly uninterested. By parental "interest" I mean an open and trusting relationship. Interrogations and spy tactics will destroy the relationship.

Marian was left to herself and as a result ended up in a clique. Children and young people are in danger when they fall in with such groups. It is almost impossible to escape their subconscious influence.

At the age of sixteen Tina came into such a group. It was only a matter of time until she adopted the attitude that young men all want to get into bed right away. Though she resisted emotionally, she submitted to this supposed natural order. Eventually she herself developed one-sided sexual needs. Her fantasies as well as her behavior were all centered on sexual satisfaction. Her supposed sexual liberation immediately led to impaired feelings of self-worth, to the point of thoughts of suicide. Later, she completely rejected her role as a woman. She wanted to be a man. But at the same time she hated men and would have been only too happy to avenge herself on them. In her daydreams, she got young men really excited only to drop them. Obviously, Tina did not use her

THE REWARDS OF TENDERNESS 97

opportunities to practice tenderness and responsibility.

Dealing with Tension
Some readers are probably impatiently waiting for an example that illustrates neither loneliness nor the influence of group sexual norms.

Victor and Michelle have known each other for a long time and can speak openly with each other about everything. They would love to move in together right away. But Michelle is still in high school and Victor has just started college. They do not yet feel that they are mature enough to marry because they are both still young. Besides, they are both still dependent on their parents for financial support.

Two people who love each other, but are not yet ready or able to marry, have many questions to discuss. "How often, how long and at what times should we see each other? Where can we meet and how can we spend the time we share? How far do we want to go in our tender physical contact? For how long should we maintain this kind of relationship? What opportunities and dangers await us?"

In spite of all their efforts to maintain a tender and responsible relationship, Victor and Michelle are noticing that it is becoming more difficult to manage the time they spend together. On the one hand, they would like to see each other as often and for as long as possible, and they love the exciting and happy evenings with candlelight and music that they spend in each other's rooms. On the other hand, they also find this closeness so fascinating that only with the greatest effort have they been able to remain true to their resolution to save physical union for marriage. Since they have petted, they feel themselves drawn more and more often onto the bed.

Let us look back to the time when their sexual relationship began to intensify. Victor's and Michelle's parents solved their obligation to supervise their children by inviting the couple into their homes. A good idea, so far. If it leads to friendly and open contact among all concerned, then tenderness and responsibility can begin to develop in shared conversations, games and plans. In Victor and Michelle's case, however, the parents had a false idea of consideration. As soon as the couple disappeared into Victor's or Michelle's room, the rule was that no family member could enter the room without first knocking. In this way the parents gave their indirect approval and encouragement for the two young people to be physically intimate.

Undoubtedly the parents liked the friend of their son or daughter, and that was why they even promoted closeness between the two young people. Yet many attractive and talented young people have stumbled into unforeseen responsibilities and obligations because of "favorable" conditions such as these. Some parents go a step further and pressure the couple to get married to protect the family's good name. If a child is on the way, young people can be forced into marriages that have little chance for success.

In the case of Victor and Michelle, their "understanding" and "accommodating" parents were to blame for their ever-growing interest in necking at the expense of shared conversation and hobbies. They sometimes had the courage to admit to themselves and to each other that these meetings behind closed doors were becoming more and more stressful. Their kisses were growing longer and more passionate. Their hands explored more and more under clothing, only to stop and leave them excited but unsatisfied. Sexual desire was moving more and more into the foreground and pushing aside the exchange of ideas that had been so lively.

All lovers have found themselves similarly torn between opposite emotions. Many couples relieve this tension by engaging in sex in spite of all its risks. Is it possible for two people to treat each other with tenderness and responsibility at the same time?

A young man wrote to me, "My girlfriend and I have agreed to

THE REWARDS OF TENDERNESS

wait. We don't know if we can wait until marriage. But we have concretely decided to leave our pants on, not to open them and to keep our hands out of them. We have drawn this line quite unromantically to avoid the greatest danger."

This young couple obviously understood the value of waiting, and both were ready to act on their conviction by making this sacrifice. They were assuming responsibility, but their decision is a stopgap measure. Their yes to waiting and their attitude toward sexuality in general seem fearful and strained. They seem to be cheating themselves of tenderness.

Is there any way for such a couple to combine responsibility and tenderness? A general rule for responsibility could be: The more clearly a couple discusses, agrees to and, of course, observes the limits of physical closeness, and the sooner they draw this line, the easier it will be for them to deal with their tension and longing. Similarly, for tenderness: The more time a couple allows for tender intellectual and emotional exchange, the more they will really get to know each other. Every shared experience leads to greater understanding of oneself and one's partner.

Such an approach emphasizes deepening and refining an erotic relationship, and not passing as quickly as possible through sexual steps to sexual satisfaction. This process of deepening their relationship is exciting for both partners. It makes them happy and leaves them free of the burden of a chronically guilty conscience. In a responsible relationship this process can and should include physical contact, with clear and mutually agreeable limits. Examples of this type of contact are a tender kiss or a loving hug. In no case should all sexuality be fearfully excluded from the relationship.

Walter Trobisch recalled many conversations with young people who were advised by their parents only that they should not "go too far" and above all not "go all the way." They never received clear and specific instructions. Out of his broad experience and countless conversations, he discovered a critical point at which both tenderness and responsibility are in immediate danger: lying down together and any form of undressing.

What have all these examples actually shown us? When one sees the ups and downs in the relationships of these young people, one can only say that the practice of tenderness and responsibility is obviously complicated. Each person and each situation is different. Nonetheless, in making a decision, consider this: the closer lovers come to petting, the greater their torment will be and the more difficult tender and responsible behavior will become!

Training in Tenderness

How then can tenderness and responsibility be learned? First, we need a trainer, one who is available and ready to act at all times. Given the absolute guidelines we have discussed, some readers may think of God. But what about people who do not believe in God? In spite of all our differences in religion, world view, nationality, sex and race, we all have something in common: a conscience. The conscience can be an excellent trainer, but we must recognize that it has a great disadvantage. It reports its findings only softly, and we can refuse to obey it at any time.

Besides a trainer, we need a training plan. It must contain specific training steps (whether or not these are put into practice will depend on the willingness of the individual). I see three important training steps: knowledge, perception and will.

The first training step is *knowledge*. Only those who know the way can start out in the right direction and avoid fatal mistakes in practicing tenderness and responsibility. It is important to know that the longing for tenderness is frequently confused with the desire for sexual satisfaction. Since everyone needs love, people quickly open their hearts when someone speaks of love. This is why many people have left themselves open to horrible abuse in the name of love. Those who recognize this misunderstanding of love are less endangered by the sexual revolution.

Obviously, it is also necessary to understand differences in sexual attitudes and behavior between males and females. In spite of plenty of available information about "sexual response curves," as well as numerous statistical reports, women often lack basic knowledge about how quickly men can become sexually excited in everyday situations. Merely seeing the picture of a woman's body or spotting a woman with sex appeal or thinking about sex can immediately trigger erotic fantasies and sexual excitement. This is a natural reflex that appears spontaneously, given an appropriate stimulus. It quickly covers up feelings of tenderness and responsibility.

Of course, women also react to erotic and sexual stimulation. But as a rule they react less intensively, and their reaction is less concentrated in the genital area. In a man, sexuality starts up right away, while in a woman the emphasis is on tenderness.

From many counseling sessions I know that women greatly underestimate this distinct difference between the sexes or are not aware of it at all. That is the only way I can explain why many women who are not looking for sexual experiences nevertheless wear clothing that is full of seductive charm—miniskirts, skintight pants or T-shirts without a bra. It is normal for these signals to awaken strong sexual desires in men.

Hardly anyone speaks out in this area. Women don't understand how men feel, and men avoid talking about it, perhaps out of fear that they will be laughed at for being weak. As a man I would like to expand on this difficult topic. Today one sees more women in pants than in dresses or skirts. Many pants are so tight that the woman's pelvic region is clearly outlined. A man can't help noticing. The same is true of see-through blouses or sheer, clinging dresses. In some cases the woman looks almost naked. I can hardly imagine that women intend to create this seductive effect. Thus, I hope that the women who are reading this book will give this some thought. It is not only a matter of showing consideration to men, but also of protecting oneself against leering looks and unwelcome attention. Some rapes could have been avoided if the women, when they bought their clothes, had considered this male sexual reflex. Simply stated, I object to the blatant sex appeal of some clothing, but I enjoy skirts and dresses that can make our world more charming, more colorful, more imaginative, warmer, softer and of course more feminine.

On the other hand, the power of sexual needs is often overestimated. Some people maintain that the sex drive, like hunger and thirst, demands satisfaction, and that people by nature are necessarily under its domination. Experience proves that notion false. We all know that a lack of food and drink can lead to grave physical disturbances, but this is not at all the case with sex. Still, some people speak of human helplessness before sexual needs. This not only is misleading, but also underestimates the uniquely human ability to control sexuality. In contrast to animals with their preprogrammed reproductive cycles, human beings can influence their sexual feelings through their will and through their behavior.

The first training step, knowledge about sexuality, is followed logically by the second—*perception*. We must become sensitive enough to perceive the difference between love as sexual desire and love as giving tenderness, not only in ourselves, but in our partners as well. Since the word *love* is ambiguous, tragic misunderstandings in a relationship can result. We can train ourselves to greater sensitivity in our perceptions by asking the following questions: Do I want to be tender or do I want sexual satisfaction? Will the longed-for physical closeness help or hurt our relationship?

Only those who have learned to perceive the differences between sexual desire and tender love are prepared to responsibly develop both tenderness and sexuality. Perception requires growing sensitivity. The girlfriend of a motorcyclist was fascinated with

THE REWARDS OF TENDERNESS

his skill and strength in controlling the heavy machine. But when he ignored her pleas and raced by a busy bus stop, almost running over a pedestrian, she discovered her boyfriend's second face: his lack of self-control and of consideration. Because she perceived this situation with sensitivity and without illusions, she was able to make a decision; she broke up with him.

The third training step is *will*. The will is the ability to make responsible decisions and to live by them. What specific decisions are necessary for the practice of tenderness and responsibility?

1. To accept oneself and one's partner.
2. To say yes to a friendship without petting and sexual intercourse.
3. To listen to one's partner and to express one's own feelings.

Some people may say, "Living by these training steps—knowledge, perception and will—is too hard! I can't do it!" This supposed inability is often invoked to avoid the necessary effort. It would be more honest to say, "I don't want to do that because it takes too much energy!" But these training steps need not strain us; we are strong enough for them. Everyone knows from experience: "What I really want to do, I do, and I make whatever effort is required!"

We have already discussed self-acceptance at the beginning of this chapter. I would like once again to emphasize the importance of accepting one's own sexuality. Men must accept that their sexual reactions are generally quicker and more intense than those of women. Self-acceptance will make men more able to discern between tenderness and sexual need, and it will make them more considerate and patient with their partners. But if they deny this difference, then they will hurt themselves and their partners through irresponsible sexual activity.

Affirmation of sex differences means also that women will take male sexuality into account and recognize their own responsibility to "put on the brakes" if necessary. At the same time they will accept their greater ability for tenderness without feeling inferior when confronted with the male sex drive. Unfortunately, too many couples perceive sex roles as a deficiency in the partner: she may think that all he ever thinks of is sex and that he has no understanding, while he accuses her of coldness or sentimentality.

It is best when each partner can enjoy his or her special characteristics as well as those of his or her partner: the feminine instinct for tenderness and the masculine interest in sex.

The second decision, to save petting and sexual intercourse for marriage, must be made by each person individually. Both are responsible for staying within the mutually agreed-upon limits. To be sure, the woman has an additional responsibility. While the man's need for tenderness overlaps with his need for sexual satisfaction, the woman can more easily distinguish between the two. Her warning light goes on much earlier: "Remember our agreement!" The woman's behavior can also help determine whether the agreed-upon limits torment the man. If she chooses to act sexy and alluring, she must remember that to play with the man's sexuality is to play with fire.

I would like to emphasize that I do not think that women are better than men, but if their ideas of love and sexuality were taken more seriously, marriages, families and society would be healthier emotionally. The man also has a great responsibility not to arouse the sexual needs of his partner too early. After marriage he can devote as much energy as he wants to making up for lost time. I know women who are very grateful to their husbands for giving them joy in their own bodies through sexual intimacy.

The third decision concerns the openness of a relationship, the willingness to express one's own feelings and to listen to those of the other. Central to this openness is the partners' frank communication about their guilt feelings and fears as well as their expectations and desires. Guilt feelings in particular are warning signals that should be neither manipulated nor ignored. They cannot be dismissed as unnecessary inhibition or immaturity. It does not matter if they are genuine and justified or false—they cannot be disregarded. Even though the official word today is that intimate relations between unmarried people are normal, most people still have subconscious guilt feelings. These cannot be talked away with logical arguments. People who engage in premarital sex feel failure and guilt—open, trusting conversations with them make this clear. The guilt feelings occur even with couples who do not become intimate until they are engaged and who later marry.

Besides the freedom to express fears, openness means opening oneself to the personality of the other. If I am going to understand him or her better, I must strongly wish to do so. I must make myself vulnerable. I must be unafraid to say something unpleasant or to share my feelings during a tender time together. The exchange between us about how we each imagine the future is also important. Are we thinking beyond our immediate friendship? If so, how?

Honest questions and honest answers can clear up misunderstandings about behavior or expectations. These conversations should cover all aspects of the relationship, particularly sexual needs and how to deal with them responsibly. An agreed-upon limit which both partners respect does not strain the relationship, but rather creates and builds trust.

Openness also has a public face. When two lovers have made a decision for one another, then people should be aware of it. The fact that a couple appears in public together is in its own way a sign of commitment and a protection for the relationship. Commitment and protection also underlie the legal and religious process of engagement and marriage.

Let us sum up this section on responsible loving. I have found that most people have one heartfelt desire for their relationship. It is not for the satisfaction of sexual needs, but for tender, compassionate love.

Those who allow themselves to be guided by their hearts have a sort of inner compass. They do not need to depend on external things such as their partner's reactions, other people's opinions, the sexual revolution and so on. Their inner compass points to independence, originality, moral courage, the willingness to take risks and responsibility. The gentle and tender giving that comes from the heart stands in stark opposition to seduction and the demand for sexual "rights."

Our hearts are sense organs for happiness. When we have a clear conscience, we also have a peaceful heart; we are contented. Thus, dissatisfaction and unrest are serious warning signals, whether for guilt, fear, anger or sadness. How fortunate it is when two people can speak openly about their feelings. Often, both discover that they have the same bad feelings when they have gone too far.

When we pay attention to the signals of our hearts, we will join tenderness and responsibility; we will begin to be responsible lovers.

Hope for the Future
9

As long as the sexual revolution rages on, clinging to the values of tenderness and responsibility seems to make as much sense as believing in fairy tales. Perhaps the speech of the fourteen-year-old boy quoted at the beginning of this book is still ringing in our ears: "I am a sexual being and want to experience this sexuality fully...." Is there room for tenderness and responsibility in today's world?

Regarding the future, world-famous authorities such as psychotherapist Carl Rogers speak of a continuing tendency toward greater freedom in sexual relationships, with young people as well as adults. Such predictions agree with the findings of many opinion polls. The future does not look rosy for tenderness and responsibility!

But there is other news as well. In the midseventies American sex researchers announced that group sex and partner swapping were passé, while love and tenderness were once again popular. Not only in America was it possible to observe a partial renunciation of liberated sexual behavior. In Sweden, the European frontrunner in the sexual revolution, similar tendencies were visible.

As we see, the experts do not agree. My optimism, however, is not based on the opinions of experts. For me, optimism is neither blind idealism nor impractical utopian thinking. Optimism is a realistic appraisal of future opportunities. When people in their everyday lives find the courage to stand up for their deepest feelings, then this optimism starts to become reality. I see opportunities for change reflected in the thoughtful and courageous attitude of many influential individuals. Realistic optimism means for me that such individuals will succeed, against the mood of the times, in their search for a new approach to sexuality and tenderness.

Here are some real-life examples of good relationships that give me hope for the future.

A pretty and well-developed young girl volunteered, "I'm proud that I still have my innocence—and I won't let anyone talk me out of it, even if people laugh at me." Her firm decision and pride are encouraging signs, because the girl lives in an unfavorable environment and spends her time with friends who have all slept with boys.

An eighteen-year-old girl with no family heeded her inner resistance to her boyfriend's advances. She perceived her own feelings, took them seriously and broke off a relationship that had already become rather serious. She did this even though it cost her several close friends. After a short time of transition, she related happily that she felt as if she had been freed from a heavy load.

A student in her early twenties had not yet had any intimate relationships; she was not "awakened" sexually. Yet she reported

HOPE FOR THE FUTURE

with no sign of shame or concern that she had no special problems with sexuality.

After several sexual experiences and changes in partners, a twenty-two-year-old woman got to know a young man who surprised her by not wanting to hop into bed right away. Her whole picture of men, that they were "only after one thing," collapsed. Some time later she wrote me, "Right now things are going pretty well for me. I still have my nice boyfriend and I hope that it stays that way for a while." After her previous bitter sexual experiences, she was obviously vacillating between fear and hope. Still, her emotional healing has begun.

A couple who had lived together for years could not decide whether to marry or to separate. Because of the problems between them, they would have separated long ago had not two fears stood as insurmountable barriers: fear of loneliness and fear of causing pain. After a hard inner struggle, they both found the courage to separate. They made this separation radically, agreeing not to contact each other indefinitely. With distance between them, they were finally able to see their true feelings.

In spite of the sexual revolution, there are couples yet today that decide to save physical union for marriage. I know this from marriages among my acquaintances. Even though some of the men studied until they were twenty-five or thirty years old and postponed marriage and sexual intimacy the whole time, I have not heard from any of them that they were harmed by waiting!

After speaking optimistically of so many individuals, let us look optimistically at our society. We have a unique opportunity to observe both the mistakes of the past, inhibitions and prudery, as well as the mistakes of the present, license and promiscuity. We can prevent one extreme from simply being followed by the other. We can learn the advantages of each, the respect for modesty and the ethical principles of earlier times combined with the free, uncomplicated attitude of today's youth.

You Can Find Tenderness!

Affirming tenderness and responsible sexuality takes hard work, but the effort pays off. It can only be made voluntarily. I would like to emphasize this voluntary nature of tenderness with the words *can* and *yes*.

I *can* be tender! (Not, I have to force myself to wait and miss out.)

I *can* assume responsibility and postpone intimate relationships! (Not, I must avoid any expression of love.)

I *can* be responsible and tender at the same time! When I act responsibly I am expressing tenderness, and when I am tender my sense of responsibility keeps me from a one-sided interest in sex.

The shortest word for voluntary consent is *yes*. It is the healthiest word in the world because it symbolizes activity and affirmation of life.

A freely spoken yes will withstand the tension resulting from sexual desires. Thus, it is possible to say a definite yes to sexuality without either completely suppressing it or completely giving in to it.

The conclusion reached in this book is not the stopping point, but the beginning of an open and honest discussion of the meaning of tenderness, responsibility and sexuality in their complex and exciting interplay. This book creates the basis for understanding. Only those people who draw the line at premarital petting and intercourse can pick up the ideas presented here and carry them further.

I hope that more and more people will find the courage to resist the spirit of the times and will independently search for tenderness. As more people do this, more attractive marriages will be made. This in turn will result in healthier families and hope for a healthier society.

One other possible way to approach this topic is found in the following chapter. I speak to Christians who rarely have trouble with the concept of responsibility, but who have a great deal of difficulty understanding tenderness and sexuality.

Christians, Tenderness and Sexuality
10

Some readers will wonder why I have included a separate chapter for Christians. I have three important reasons.

First, I frequently observe Christians who have trouble with their attitudes about tenderness and, above all, sexuality. Either they are antiphysical and prudish, or they abuse Christian freedom by seeking to explain away obvious sexual immorality as a manifestation of love.

Second, Christians and particularly theologians seem uncertain about whether the Bible gives any guiding principles about premarital relations.

Third, many young Christians suffer because they have no examples to follow. Many do not know of a single person in their circle of friends who plans to wait until marriage.

Finally, I have a personal reason. I do not want to rely entirely on the logical and psychological arguments offered by my profession as counselor and psychotherapist. Rather, as a Christian I also want to carefully consider biblical teaching and pastoral practice.

The Bible's attitude toward sexuality is clear, but not all Christians have healthy attitudes. Christians need to learn how to effectively minister to each other in this area. If they do, Christians have a solid basis for optimism. The prerequisite for understanding Christian ministry is the experience of being a Christian. I do hope, however, that this chapter will cause some non-Christian readers to reflect on the Christian faith. The theological statements can be verified at any time by any reader with the help of a Bible.

Sexuality in Scripture

Although few parts of the Bible concern themselves specifically with intimate relations between unmarried people, there are numerous passages on love in both Old and New Testaments. In addition, there are several clear statements about virginity until marriage. These few places are totally unambiguous. I suspect there are not more such passages because in biblical times sexual abstinence before marriage was taken for granted.

Before looking at these specific passages, we should create a frame of reference for them. All of God's commandments must be seen against the background of his all-encompassing offer of love.

How does this offer relate to sexuality? I see three ways: God affirms our physical nature, he gives us all the prerequisites for experiencing love, and he blesses marriage in a special way.

In contrast to the antiphysical attitude in some Christian circles, God says a clear yes to our body and to our sexuality. In an argument with the Pharisees Christ expressly says, "He who made them from the beginning made them male and female, and said 'For this reason a man shall leave his father and mother and be joined to his wife, and the two shall become one flesh' " (Mt 19:4-5). As numerous entries in any concordance point out, the body has great significance in the Bible. Paul reminded the Corinthians that their body was a "temple of the Holy Spirit" (1 Cor 6:19). He did not use the word *body* in a spiritualized sense; rather he put this sentence between a warning against immorality (1 Cor 6:12-18) and a detailed admonition about attitudes toward sexuality in marriage: "For the wife does not rule over her own body, but the husband does; likewise the husband does not rule over his own body, but the wife does. Do not refuse one another except perhaps by agreement for a season" (1 Cor 7:4-5).

In addition, everyone can read the frank discussions in the Bible of the sexual shortcomings of many "men of the faith." Behavior such as adultery, homosexuality and fornication is mentioned specifically. These explicit reports of sexual misbehavior are so realistic in the Old Testament that as a student in confirmation class I methodically looked them up and devoured them with great interest. Those who still hold the mistaken opinion that the Bible is antiphysical should read the Song of Solomon in which the bridegroom's joy over his bride's body—and her joy over his—is clearly expressed.

Central to our frame of reference is love. Love is the pivotal concept of Christianity. It is also the best characterization of God. "God is love" (1 Jn 4:16) is the most important message of the gospel. When we read the well-known love chapter, 1 Corinthians 13, we can begin to understand what God means by love. I will quote sentences that are directly related to tenderness and sexuality: "Love is patient" (it has endurance and can wait); "it is not arrogant or rude" (compare Phil 1:10); "love does not insist on its own way" (it is not selfishly interested only in the satisfaction of its own needs); and it "rejoices in the right" (it does not pass over the boundary it has set between right and wrong behavior, and it finds joy in this affirmation of right living).

Love and sexuality find their special meaning in marriage. By marriage the New Testament means monogamy (1 Cor 7:2: "Each man should have his own wife and each woman her own husband"). Because this form of marriage is ordained by God, Jesus says, "What therefore God has joined together, let not man put asunder" (Mt 19:6).

Marriage is highly esteemed in the Bible. Frequently marriage is used as a metaphor of the close relationship between God and man: for example, Jesus is called the "bridegroom," and the Christian church, the "bride" (2 Cor 11:2). Marriage is even seen as new creation: "So they are no longer two but one flesh" (Mt 19:6). This unity of man and woman in marriage cannot be expressed mathematically. Even though according to human calculation one partner plus one partner equals two partners, as far as God is concerned, the sum is one!

This is only a rough sketch of the wondrous offer of love God makes to those who turn to him. Such an offer must be protected against abuse. That is why God gave his commandments—as guideposts for life. They serve the same purpose as the sign at the top of a cliff that says, "Caution—danger ahead!"

Behind every one of God's demands is his offer of love. This offer should cause people to obey their loving Father out of love. Each commandment could add, "Because you know that I am your God and that I love you, you will keep this commandment!"

In the Sermon on the Mount (Mt 5—7) Jesus does not abolish a single iota or dot of the Old Testament commandments; rather he actually renews them with a special interpretation. Of sexuality he says, "You have heard it was said, 'You shall not commit adultery.' But I say to you that everyone who looks at a woman lustfully has already committed adultery with her in his heart" (Mt 5:27-28). Jesus' resistance to sexual possessiveness goes beyond observable sexual misbehavior to the thoughts of the heart. Thus I am certain that Jesus also totally rejects possessiveness as manifested in premarital sex. Although we have no record that Jesus ever expressly took a position on premarital sex, we must not close our eyes to the intellectual and emotional standard he set nor to the clear teaching of the rest of Scripture.

Into our theological frame of reference, which includes both God's offer and his commandments, we can fit the specific question of which biblical passages address the topic of premarital sex. The Old Testament clearly shows that God is serious about his regulations concerning sexual contact between men and women —deadly serious, in fact. That is the only way we can understand the following passage: "If a man is found lying with the wife of another man, both of them shall die, the man who lay with the woman, and the woman; so you shall purge the evil from Israel" (Deut 22:22).

Even after the wedding night a man could accuse his wife before the elders of the city if he discovered that she had had sex beforehand: "But if the thing is true, that the tokens of virginity were not found in the young woman, then they shall bring out the young woman to the door of her father's house, and the men of her city shall stone her to death with stones, because she has wrought folly in Israel by playing the harlot in her father's house" (Deut 22:20-21).

If a premarital relationship was discovered, the Old Testament recommended immediate marriage: "If a man meets a virgin who is not betrothed, and seizes her and lies with her, and they are found, then . . . she shall be his wife, because he has violated her; he may not put her away all his days" (Deut 22:28-29).

These Old Testament regulations may be new to many people, but here is a passage familiar to all of us from the wedding ceremony: "Therefore a man leaves his father and his mother and cleaves to his wife, and they become one flesh" (Gen 2:24). This sentence clearly tells which steps follow which in a serious relationship: first leaving one's parents, then marrying, and only then having physical union!

The teaching of the Old Testament is clear. Sexual relations are inseparable from marriage.

This part of God's will also holds true for the New Testament. Paul writes to the church in Thessalonica: "For this is the will of God, your sanctification: that you abstain from unchastity; that each one of you know how to take a wife for himself in holiness and honor not in the passion of lust like heathen who do not know God" (1 Thess 4:3-5). And to the church in Corinth, he directs: "If [the unmarried] cannot exercise self-control, then they should marry. For it is better to marry than to be aflame with passion" (1 Cor 7:9).

Thus, according to the understanding of the Christian church, physical union is reserved exclusively for marriage. For Paul there are only two possibilities: to remain unmarried and abstain from sexual relations, or to marry. To compromise by allowing sexual relations between unmarried adults is so unthinkable for Paul that he does not even mention the possibility. To the contrary, he labels all extramarital intimate relations as immorality. Passionately he admonishes the Corinthians to "shun immorality" (1 Cor 6:18). To the Thessalonians he writes: "Abstain from unchastity" (1 Thess 4:3). We are all startled by these ugly words *immorality* and *unchastity*. They have a "holier than thou" ring to them. But sexual behavior is obviously so important to God that no word is too strong to be used in warning people of the danger: "For God has not called us for uncleanness, but in holiness" (1 Thess 4:7). And Paul warns, "Therefore whoever disregards this, disregards not man but God" (1 Thess 4:8).

Abstinence before marriage was so clearly understood and taken for granted by the early church that even engaged couples adhered strictly to this rule. This is the only way to explain 2 Corinthians 11:2, where Paul describes the church of Corinth as a "pure bride" who was "betrothed" to Jesus.

The fact that premarital chastity was taken for granted is illustrated by a well-known Bible story. Mary and Joseph were engaged when the coming birth of Jesus was announced to Mary. As a virgin, Mary must have been shocked to learn that she would soon be pregnant (Lk 1:26-38). For this reason her acceptance was a truly unbelievable sacrifice. Out of trust and obedience to God she risked her entire future existence. She had to accept the likelihood of a broken engagement and shame and the possibility of stoning. For Joseph as well, the absolute rule, "No intimate relations until marriage," was binding. He was in complete despair. From the human point of view the only explanation was that his fiancée had been unfaithful. Because he loved Mary and because he was a "just man," he decided not to publicize the matter but to "divorce her quietly" (Mt 1:19). Only God's intervention in a dream prevented tragedy.

If we try to empathize with Mary and Joseph, we can feel something of their tragic desperation. But it can be understood only on the basis of a clear separation between the abstinent engagement period and marriage.

In summary, the Bible's teaching in both Old and New Testaments clearly prohibits premarital sexual intimacy. As far as the Bible is concerned, no theological uncertainty exists. It is sad when the Bible's clarity is obscured by making the concept *love* so ambiguous that it can easily be misunderstood and abused by anyone.

Christian Problems

In spite of the Bible's clarity about God's offer and his commands, many Christians have serious problems in dealing with their personal sexuality on a practical level.

"Ecclesiastical neurosis" is the malady of those Christians who cannot cope with sexuality, but try to deny or suppress it. Their attitude drives them to an inhibited and prudish legalism, and they frequently condemn those around them. Anything that can be associated even remotely with eroticism or sexuality is an evil to avoid at all costs.

It is no surprise that such a negation of the body can lead to serious disturbances, sometimes to total sexual inhibition and escape into a fantasy world, sometimes to masturbation and finally an explosive escape from inhibition. Young people who are raised with strict religious taboos often try to break out at the first opportunity in order to make up for lost time. Tenderness is necessarily sold short.

Christian prudery does not pay off—but neither does the opposite extreme: the apparently happy and uncomplicated practice of sexual relations outside marriage. Christians who act this way abuse the biblical offer of love and physical affirmation. They also have a false picture of guilt and forgiveness. They may speak of God in personal terms yet openly promote their liberated attitudes about sexuality. Some unmarried Christians have manipulated their consciences to the point that they claim to feel no guilt over engaging in sex in a serious relationship or during engagement. When such Christians pay attention neither to biblical teaching nor to the admonition of other Christians, their behavior deteriorates. A young woman who was having an affair with a married man told me that she had no guilt feelings whatsoever and that she could give an account of this affair to herself and to "her God" at any time. She was obviously convinced of the validity of her behavior and considered herself a progressive Christian.

Unfortunately some pastors share this attitude, and it is tragic when they are well known and influential. An experienced pastoral counselor told me that he had sexual relations with a counselee and then encouraged her to enter a lesbian relationship with her girlfriend. This "minister" had the audacity—or blindness—to maintain that his behavior and advice were in harmony with the Bible! Perhaps he was convinced that his sexual behavior made him a messenger of "brotherly love."

Those who hear such examples can only be amazed at how much self-deception, rationalization, denial and conscience-manipulation Christians are capable of.

My ministerial experience has shown me that an unhealthy attitude toward sexuality is an unsolved problem for many Christians. Many Christian groups advocate prudery; others pursue sexual liberty. Both attitudes are unattractive to those outside the Christian community. Thus, the Christian teaching itself becomes unattractive and loses credibility. Between the good news on the one hand and its practice on the other, there is sometimes a wide gap. It is reasonable to ask why we see this discrepancy between biblical teaching and everyday behavior.

The main problem is *subjectivism*—the mistaken attitude of many Christians who base their decisions and their behavior on their own feelings rather than on the will of God. Both the adulterous young woman and the fornicating pastor rely entirely on their feelings and on "their" God. They try to defend such subjectivism with the reproachful question, Can love be sin? The question assumes a negative answer. The mere mention of the clear biblical teaching meets with stiff resistance.

It is tragic that many Christians do not make an effort to discover God's will. This ignorance borders on criminal recklessness. God offers us the only absolutes that exist. Besides his objective truth, everything in our world is relative and subjective. God's truth consists of his offers and commandments. Those who ignore his boundaries place their entire lives in jeopardy.

Closely related to subjectivism is the psychological fad of *self-actualization*. From a psychotherapeutic point of view, it is good when a passive, depressive or aggressive person decides to take personal responsibility for his or her self-improvement. But for many people self-actualization becomes the magic key to a new philosophy of life, or even a replacement for religion. In any case, self and not God is the focus of self-actualization. This is normal for non-Christians. Those with no relationship to God have no other choice but to rely on their own feelings and to put faith in their own self-actualization.

It is sad, however, when Christians adopt this philosophy, because it leads to rejecting God's guidance. These people try to live a Christian life, but rely on themselves rather than God. Their desire to make it alone is automatically accompanied by independence from the God of love, who can build on our trust but never on our self-glorification. According to the Bible all people who live their lives without God are blind. It is possible for such blind people to be active in a church and to appear deeply interested in matters of faith, but religious self-actualization is reminiscent of the "justification by works" that Paul attacked so sharply.

I hope my intention is clear. I do not wish to condemn, but rather to point out misunderstandings in the so-called Christian lifestyle of some people. It is my concern that these dislocated norms be put back in place by a direct confrontation with the will of God, the gospel, the good news of freedom, peace and joy.

The ministry of committed Christians can be a valuable aid in restoring the fundamental values of life.

Helping Christians Find Tenderness

Ministry is probably known to most Christians only in the sense of the "minister" as "pastor." I wish to use the word *ministry* in a broader way. Ministry is the loving, open and direct conversation between a Christian who is seeking advice and one who is helping (ministering). These two Christians need to bear in mind that they are not merely participating in a human conversation, but are also in the presence of the resurrected Christ who said of himself, "Where two or three are gathered in my name, there am I in the midst of them" (Mt 18:20). Unfortunately, this vitally important kind of ministry has been more and more ignored in the course of church history and has only recently come back into practice in some Christian groups.

Ministry is possible only when both the individual—or couple—seeking help, as well as the one who is ministering, takes God's offer and his commandment seriously. Obedience to God's commandment has nothing to do with groaning under an unbearable load, the alleged cross of some Christians. Instead, obedience is a sign of the genuine trust of Christians in their Father's loving training. This is why a Christian "delights in his commandments" (Ps 112:1) and finds that trust in God does not lead to pain. On the contrary, God responds to a Christian's obedience by blessing his or her life.

We can understand what it means to take God's commandment and offer seriously by looking at two central concepts of the Christian faith: love and commitment.

The word *love* occurs often in the Bible. It includes both God's offer of love and his commandment to love. The love commandment is in three of the four Gospels: "You shall love the Lord your God with all your heart, and with all your soul, and with all your mind. This is the great and first commandment. And a second is like it, You shall love your neighbor as yourself" (Mt 22:37-39). Not only because of its frequency (compare corresponding passages in Lev 19:18; Deut 6:5; Mk 12:30-31; Lk 10:27) is this commandment of special importance, but also because of Jesus' evaluation: "On these two commandments depend all the law and the prophets" (Mt 22:40).

Jesus emphasizes the equal importance of loving God, one's neighbor and oneself. We have already discussed at length the meaning of loving oneself and loving one's neighbor, but not of loving God. This commandment's importance is emphasized by its forceful presentation. It demands commitment of the whole person to God: our entire heart, our entire soul, our entire strength and our entire mind. Commitment, like love, is a central concept of the Christian faith. Jesus evaluated commitment highly: "He who loses his life for my sake will find it" (Mt 10:39). This paradoxical sentence tells what commitment means: to forgo our selfish possessiveness and independence, to be willing to let go of everything that is dear to our hearts, and to make Jesus the center of our lives.

When I give up self-actualization for Jesus' sake, then something decisive happens. There is a change of leadership. Self voluntarily makes room for Jesus in the heart. This momentous decision, this act of commitment, takes place as an act of will independent of the current emotional state. God takes our conscious commitment very seriously and does not hesitate in responding. He gives us everything we need so that instead of losing we gain much. We find a purposeful and fulfilled life, something we almost lost through our own efforts at self-actualization.

Commitment gives every Christian an opportunity to see the power of God in all areas of their lives: school, profession, family, hobby, tenderness and responsibility, and even sexuality.

Obviously I can commit only something that I already have. I can place my sexuality under the lordship of Christ only when I have accepted my body. But when I commit my sexuality to God, I must be truly prepared to give it up, rather than live for it as is common today. Those who give up their claim to sexual satisfaction and surrender their needs completely to God have a life-changing experience. Under God's influence and leading, desiring love is transformed into giving love.

Of course commitment does not solve all problems. We live in a world full of exciting possibilities and a great many temptations as well. But a Christian receives "spiritual weapons" that he can use successfully. Prayer, for instance, whether thanking God for another person or asking for a blessing on him or her, automatically filters lust out of the relationship and defuses the desire for sexual possession. A life of prayer does not lead to impoverishment and boredom, but rather to greater inner freedom and joy in contacts between men and women.

With these thoughts on love and commitment as a basis, let us discuss concrete questions and problems that Christians may have in the area of premarital sex.

Guidelines for Christian Behavior

Are there any guiding principles for Christians when it comes to choosing a life's partner? In answering this question, I want to make two important points. First, the prospective partner should also be a Christian, because Christianity is not a private hobby but a commitment to God and an attitude toward life. Second, it is also important to know if this relationship is in accordance with God's will. This can be determined through silent communication with God and through discussion with other Christians or with a pastor in particular.

Inner unrest is an alarm signal for any type of behavior that is not acceptable from God's point of view. Augustine recognized the meaning of unrest when he wrote, "Our heart is restless until it rests in you." Christian couples who wish to treat each other responsibly and lovingly should ask, "Is our desire for tenderness and physical closeness in accordance with God's will or does it make us feel guilty?" We can be contented only when we are in harmony with God. A restless heart is generally a warning against disobedience or a signal of guilt. There is no simple way to distinguish between genuine and false guilt feelings, but we should take even vague feelings seriously rather than disregard them as signs of a prudish upbringing or backwardness in society. The most important question in examining ourselves is: "Do we feel at peace about what we are doing or planning?"

Christians should also pay attention to those around them.

Though we are ultimately responsible only to Jesus for our behavior, we must also consider the effect our friendship might have on others. As disciples of Jesus we Christians are carefully watched by those around us. We can understand Peter's concern when he wrote, "Beloved, I beseech you as aliens and exiles to abstain from the passions of the flesh that wage war against your soul. Maintain good conduct among the Gentiles" (1 Pet 2:11-12).

Even though the people around us generally take no critical notice of premarital sex, it is quite another matter when the people involved in it are Christians. Even non-Christians suspect that Christianity and premarital intimacy do not go together. They may respond with a wide range of feelings—gloating, anger, sadness, disappointment. In any case the clarity and credibility of the gospel suffer.

Here are three typical situations that call for ministry between Christians.

The first situation is the simplest because neither member of the couple in question has had sexual relations, and the partners are only beginning to consider how far to go in physical intimacy. Both must ask themselves to what extent their desire for tenderness and physical closeness is in harmony with God. They must avoid situations and activities that would make self-control difficult, specifically, viewing suggestive films, drinking alcoholic beverages and being alone together too much. Paul's advice could help such Christians: "Put on the Lord Jesus Christ, and make no provision for the flesh, to gratify its desires" (Rom 13:14).

The second situation, when the couple feels ready for sexual intercourse, is more difficult. The ministering person should confront both of them with their previous behavior which has led to this longing for physical union.

The couple may have reached the point where further waiting would be torment. The ministering person must help them find a solution. There are only two possibilities: marriage or abstinence.

Paul gives a brief justification for the first solution: "For it is better to marry than to be aflame with passion" (1 Cor 7:9). The counselor and the couple must carefully examine whether they are old enough and mature enough to marry.

The second solution is appropriate when both members of the couple are young. It is especially important that both of them agree to wait. This way is doubtless difficult and possible only if both partners are willing to exercise honest self-examination and responsible tenderness—in close cooperation with the ministering person. They should agree to avoid sexually exciting situations as much as possible. They may need to make decisive changes in their behavior: for example, no longer going to each other's room to be alone. It could even make sense for one of them to move to a different community until they are ready to marry.

If the counselor is too soft, too sympathetic and too subjective, he or she will be unable to help because all these solutions are painful to some extent. Unfortunately, some counselors have "progressed" so far that they tolerate premarital intimacy between engaged people either expressly or as a last resort. This is dangerous. Well-intentioned counsel of this type can cause great harm, not only the kind described at length in this book, but also the worst harm that can come to a Christian: a life of disobedience to God. Such a life is robbed of peace and joy and communion with God.

Another danger is that subjective advice can become a welcome excuse for people who find the "rules" too strict and inhumane. An engaged couple, both Christians, were given very permissive counsel by their pastor. They were incautious and thoughtless enough to talk about it with others. Another Christian who was involved in a completely different relationship heard this advice. This "pastoral blessing" was all he needed to rid himself of his last reservations against sexual intimacy.

In my opinion there is never a good reason to depart from the biblical guidelines. This holds even for divorced and widowed people who may have particular difficulties when they begin a relationship with a new partner. Since their previous marriage has given them sexual experience and they are now hungry for love, the renewed practice of patience and responsible tenderness can be extremely hard. But even in this difficult case, obedience to God's commandment is the only reasonable and helpful decision. Anything else will bring unrest. The situation is even more problematic when there are children present to observe any disobedience and immorality of their parent and automatically incorporate it into their own attitudes on friendship, love and marriage.

If the only possible solution for a couple is to wait, then the ministering person should encourage them to practice tenderness and responsibility. If the counselor thinks too much in human terms and does not put enough trust in God's love and care, then he or she will rob the couple of their only true support and will share the responsibility and guilt for their decision.

The final situation involves ministry after an unmarried couple has had intimate relations. In this case, as in the others, there are only two choices: marriage or abstinence. The ministering person must resist the temptation to take the existing state of affairs for granted and to give approval for it in the future. He or she should make the couple aware of the possible danger and open their eyes to what they are risking. If both members of the couple then decisively agree to one of the two solutions, a genuine new beginning is possible.

In all counseling, the ministering person must advise and assist lovingly. He or she is God's representative and presents God's offer of grace and forgiveness. Without love, responsibility becomes coldness, justice is brutal, and even the most subtle insight is dogmatism.

It is possible for the ministering person to cause pain by telling the truth in love. The ministering person who presents God's commandments, however, must speak of obedience in the attractive terms of God's offer of love and forgiveness. To minister is to sympathize and understand. Accepting another person has nothing to do with approving his or her attitudes or behavior. With all compassion the counselor represents God's limits as revealed in the Bible. Ministry creates an atmosphere of Christian hope.

Christian Hope

I would like to speak once again of optimism, this time in the context of Christian hope. Next to faith and love, hope is the third foundation stone of the Christian life (see 1 Cor 13:13).

By *hope* I do not mean "taking comfort in the hereafter." Some Christians adopt this attitude all too quickly, either displaying aggressive hostility to "the world" or retreating into depression, resignation and negativism. Paul wanted to hear nothing of such escapism. In his letter to Titus he wrote, "For the grace of God has appeared for the salvation of all men, training us to renounce irreligion and worldly passions, and to live sober, upright, and godly lives in this world" (Tit 2:11-12).

In addition to the hope of eternal life, Christian hope means the chance to experience peace, joy and freedom in our everyday lives. This offer is especially directed to those who struggle with serious or threatening problems, above all, guilt. Dealing with sexuality quickly brings many people to the borders of failure and guilt. But no one need lose hope. Forgiveness is a reality—I can confirm this in my own life. Christian faith and trust give strength to crisis situations, making people ready and willing to bring every type of guilt to Jesus as soon as possible and to thankfully accept forgiveness.

During Germany's Third Reich, Dietrich Bonhoeffer, an outstanding witness for Christianity and hope, paid for his witness with his life. In his book *Letters and Papers from Prison* he offers his thoughts on the word *optimism,* which he understood to mean

"Christian hope." Bonhoeffer's words hang as a motto in my counseling room:

> Optimism... is the inspiration of life and hope when others give in; it enables a man to hold his head high when everything seems to be going wrong; it gives him strength to sustain reverses and yet to claim the future for himself instead of abandoning it to his opponent. It is true that there is a silly, cowardly kind of optimism, which we must condemn. But the optimism that is will for the future should never be despised, even if it is proved wrong a hundred times; it is health and vitality, and the sick man has no business to impugn it. There are people who regard it as frivolous, and some Christians think it impious for anyone to hope and prepare for a better earthly future. They think that the meaning of present events is chaos, disorder, and catastrophe; and in resignation or pious escapism they surrender all responsibility for reconstruction and for future generations. It may be that the day of judgment will dawn tomorrow; in that case, we shall gladly stop working for a better future. But not before. [Ed. Eberhard Bethge, enlarged edition (New York: Macmillan Paperbacks, 1972), pp. 15-16]

These sentences, written in prison, represent a courageous "nevertheless." They represent the serious side of Christian hope, the responsible readiness to intervene for a better future. We can all work toward a better future by working toward two goals: (1) the establishment of tenderness as a weapon against both prudery and license, and (2) the acceptance of love as the basis of sexuality.

We need to consider the future as we struggle on two fronts, against the sex-advocates and need-ideologists on the one hand, and the prudish moralists and teachers of the law on the other. The first group irresponsibly disregards clear biblical and interpersonal rules, and closes its eyes to many risks. The second group, on the other hand, clings to antiphysical attitudes even though they are unbiblical and unchristian.

The other side of Christian hope is joy. I am discovering more and more decidedly happy Christian marriages. Simply the fact that there are many examples of strong Christian marriages and families is a reason to hope.

"We have been married for fifteen years and have seven children," one couple told Walter Trobisch. "Our marriage and our family are very happy." They recalled that with their pastor's help they had decided to save sexual intimacy for marriage. On their wedding night they saw each other naked for the first time and began to discover together the whole spectrum of tenderness and sexuality. This couple's approach is well illustrated by a figure of speech that is common in India and Africa. At their marriage this couple put a relatively cold pot on the marriage fire and found that from year to year the contents became hotter. Some Indians and Africans note that in Europe and America, when people marry they often take a boiling pot off the fire and put it in the ashes, so that it becomes colder and colder as time passes.

I know a retired couple who share obvious love, respect and reverence for each other. Each has a distinct personality, and yet they take great joy in their unity that transcends the equation one plus one equals two. Their life shows us younger people that marriage is a precious and particularly loving gift of God.

The more examples, the more rays of light there are in this world, the more probable it becomes that love and responsibility will once again meet. Once again people will be able to enjoy a lively mingling of tenderness, love, intimacy, amorousness, passion, eroticism and sexuality, each in its season.

The Tenderness of Jesus
In our search for examples we cannot ignore the greatest of all: Jesus! Jesus is so inspiring that even for non-Christians he exemplifies humanistic and social ideals.

The love of Jesus joins all imaginable opposites in a unified whole. Jesus preached tenderness as well as responsibility. The love he lived out before us was never sweetly sentimental as represented in some portraits with their transfigured smiles. Jesus' love rebukes those people who insist on a one-sided point of view, whether license or prudery. In contrast to license, Jesus' love is responsible; in contrast to prudery, it is tender.

The spectrum of Jesus' love is too wide for some people. Because some of his statements seem to contradict one another, he (like the Bible) may be called inconsistent. But Jesus had the courage to express himself clearly, in warning or in consolation according to the situation and the individual. His differentiated ministry is consistent and always on target!

Though love is Jesus' central theme, it is not to be associated with dimestore caricatures of the "sweet little Jesus." Jesus' love meant that he caused pain. His personality seems hard in comparison with our soft understanding of "Christian." He hurled the word *Satan* at the apostle Peter, the "rock" of the Christian church, when pity moved Peter to restrain Jesus from suffering as the Savior must (Mt 16:23). Jesus was openly angry with his disciples: "O faithless and perverse generation, ... how long am I to bear with you?" (Mt 17:17).

Jesus spoke plainly to the Pharisees, the theologians of that day, when he unashamedly called them "hypocrites," "serpents" and "vipers" (Mt 23:1-36). He physically threw the moneychangers out of the temple (Mt 21:12). Jesus had a strong self-concept. He frequently used the phrase "I am" to refer to his authority as the Son of God. What dignity, what seriousness and what love stand behind his claim: "I am the way, and the truth, and the life; no one comes to the Father, but by me" (Jn 14:6)!

Better known than the strict side of Jesus' love are his mercy and grace. We see this in the numerous reports of healings. The same love made it possible for Jesus to set himself above the unwritten social laws in order to speak lovingly and without inhibition to the untouchables of his time, the tax collectors and prostitutes.

For Jesus, forgiving sin was more important than healing disease. His forgiving love is seen in his meeting with an adulteress, whom he was able to save from stoning. He challenged each of the law-bound men present to examine his own conscience: "Let him who is without sin among you be the first to throw a stone at her" (Jn 8:7). This dramatic event ends with Jesus' ministering to the adulteress and forgiving her sin.

He was also tender and caring in his treatment of his disciples and his mother. John was allowed to rest on his breast (Jn 13:23). Even in the hour of his death he brought his mother and his disciple John together. Thus we see that Jesus was full of tenderness, but that he could also respond sternly, according to his evaluation of the situation and the person with whom he was speaking.

Did Jesus limit himself to brotherly love? How does he stand with respect to love for God and love for himself?

His love for God is confirmed by the many passages in the Gospels where Jesus prays lovingly and trustingly to his Father. Sometimes Jesus addresses his Father with the familiar name *Abba* (Mk 14:36), which can be freely translated *Papa* or *Daddy*.

Applying the term *self-love* to Jesus may seem strange to us at first, especially when we think of his selfless life, suffering and death. But Jesus paid attention to himself and to his needs. He frequently wished to be alone and undisturbed with his Father. He also enjoyed eating and drinking, so much so that his opponents called him a "glutton and drunkard" (Mt 11:19).

Jesus could express tender feelings openly. He wept when he heard of the death of his friend Lazarus (Jn 11:35), and he enjoyed being with children. Mark relates that "he took them in his arms" (Mk 10:16). Jesus had a completely natural and uncomplicated relationship with women. He was friends with the two sisters of Lazarus (Jn 11:5), and he justified the tenderness of the sinful woman who "wet his feet with her tears," "wiped them with the hair of her head," and kissed and anointed them with expensive ointment (Lk 7:38).

My education and profession have helped in my personal development and in my marriage and family. But the significant corrections at critical turning points in my life came through the Bible and the ministry of others. I am one hundred per cent convinced that there is no better offer and no more protective commandment for us as human beings than what we find in the Word of God. The more seriously and concretely I accept God's norms in my everyday decisions, the greater my interest in Jesus and my thankfulness to God.

I hope that by responsibly affirming sexuality, you too will fulfill your longing for tenderness and will find the opportunity to meet Jesus.

Recommended Reading from InterVarsity Press

Eros Defiled. John White maintains compassion for the person struggling in the areas of premarital and extramarital sex, homosexuality and masturbation, offering forgiveness and a way out. 172 pages, paper

Growing into Love. Joyce Huggett looks at questions faced by couples who are just beginning to face issues of commitment, engagement and marriage, giving a sound Christian perspective to problems of love, choosing, expectations, sex, roles and parenthood. 128 pages, paper

A Handbook for Engaged Couples. Robert and Alice Fryling offer engaged couples a communication tool covering such topics as handling money and time, solving problems together, dealing with family relationships and planning the wedding and honeymoon. 72 pages, paper

How Do You Say, "I Love You"? Judson J. Swihart helps married couples unravel the complexities of saying and hearing "I love you" through a discussion of eight different languages of love. 96 pages, paper

Living with Unfulfilled Desires. Walter Trobisch counsels teen-agers who are just learning to cope with their own unfulfilled sexual desires. 128 pages, paper

Love Is a Feeling to Be Learned. Walter Trobisch explores the mystery of love—its tension and fulfillment, its deep longing and hostility, its beauty and burden. 37 pages, paper

Love Yourself. Walter Trobisch, in a warm, personal and practical book, discusses the relationship between self-love and self-hate, self-acceptance and self-rejection. 55 pages, paper

My Beautiful Feeling. Walter and Ingrid Trobisch, in a series of actual letters, counsel Ilona in the area of masturbation, a constantly recurring issue in the Trobisches' ministry. 128 pages, paper

Single and Human. Ada Lum tells how a single person can lead a full and happy life, resolving inner sexual tensions and feelings of inferiority and frustration. 82 pages, paper

Two into One. Joyce Huggett helps newlyweds and those contemplating marriage by offering biblical advice on marriage vows, listening and communicating, love and submission, prayer, ministry to others, sex, and conflict. 128 pages, paper